Foreword

At 11:02 on the day of August 9, 1945, the city of Nagasaki was instantly destroyed by a single atomic bomb. The number of casualties rose to approximately 70,000 people, which was one third of the citizenship at the time. The victims included elderly people, women and innocent children. Those who managed to survive were afflicted by a variety of ailments including wounds from the blast and heat rays of the bomb, illnesses caused by radiation exposure, and mental anguish brought on by the trauma experienced on that day. Their suffering persists right up until the present.

Our facility, the Nagasaki National Peace Memorial Hall for the Atomic Bomb Victims, was created for the purpose of spreading the truth about the atomic bombings to as many people as possible in both Japan and countries around the world. We work to ensure that such information is passed on to future generations, and to provide a memorial for eternal peace. Photographs of the deceased and written memoirs are displayed so that visitors may come to understand the reality of the atomic bombings and the importance of peace through the words and feelings of individual survivors. For the publication of "The Light of Morning- Memoirs of the Nagasaki Atomic Bomb Survivors", we have selected nine of the personal accounts from our collection.

Nagasaki and Hiroshima are the only places in the world that have experienced the tragic consequences of atomic bombings. From these two cities, along with the entire country of Japan, pleas for world peace and the elimination of nuclear weapons at the earliest possible date are constantly being made. The actual experiences of those who witnessed the atomic bombings have always formed the cornerstone of these pleas. With the number of survivors who can speak of their experiences declining year by year, those of us who live in the atomic-bombed cities feel that it is our mission to carry on their work, and to send out to the world their message that these tragedies must never be repeated.

"May Nagasaki be the last place on earth to experience an atomic bombing…"

We will be extremely pleased if this book gives readers even the slightest insight into the appeal of the atomic bomb survivors.

Lastly, we would like to extend our gratitude to all whose efforts helped bring this book to completion, especially the authors of the original memoirs.

The Director of the Nagasaki National Peace Memorial Hall for the Atomic Bomb Victims

May, 2005

May 17, 2017
Nagasaki

The Light of Morning

Memoirs of the Nagasaki Atomic Bomb Survivors

The Light of Morning:
Memoirs of the Nagasaki Atomic Bomb Survivors

Printed in May, 2005
Nagasaki National Peace Memorial Hall
for the Atomic Bomb Victims
Translated by Brian Burke-Gaffney

852-8117 Nagasaki-shi, Hirano-machi 7-8, Japan
Tel: +81(0)95-814-0055
Fax: +81(0)95-814-0056
http://www.peace-nagasaki.go.jp
e-mail:info@peace-nagasaki.go.jp

ISBN 4-9902545-0-3

Contents

A Week of Horror and Human Love

Tatsuichiro Akizuki

Tatsuichiro Akizuki (center) in 1946

August 9

One hot summer day followed another. Every night like clockwork I was aroused from sleep by an air-raid alarm near midnight. People had been trembling in fear for months, each day wondering if this would be the day of destruction by an air raid, but oddly enough Nagasaki remained unscathed.

On August 5 or 6 a rumor circulated, source unknown, that Nagasaki would soon be reduced to ashes. Local leaders denounced this as a plot by subversive elements to delude the people of Nagasaki, but the ominous rumor left a residue of unease in the corner of people's minds.

On August 6 I heard the news that a "new-type bomb" had been dropped on Hiroshima. This was one of the most noteworthy events in the history of humanity, but army authorities brushed over it, reporting simply that the bomb had caused considerable damage in the city.

The sun was shining brightly again on the morning of August 9. There were 58 inpatients and 20 outpatients at the hospital. An engineer at the nearby Mitsubishi Arms Factory, who had come for treatment, told me about the new-type bomb. He said that the bomb dropped on Hiroshima had probably harnessed atomic power and conjectured that, if so, it would wield enough destructive force to push humankind to the brink of extinction.

Just when we were speaking, close to eleven o'clock, the air-raid sirens began to wail. The engineer left the hospital in a rush, and I went out into the garden to check on things. There was not a speck of cloud in the sky. After a few minutes the sirens relented. Back in the clinic, I began a pneumothorax procedure on a young man of about 20 years old, slipping a needle into his chest cavity. Dr. Kimura and Dr. Hakataya from Takahara Hospital were standing behind me along with two nurses, Ms. Murai and Ms. Kajiyama.

Suddenly, a loud buzzing sound echoed overhead. I pulled out the needle and shouted, "Someone take watch!" By the time Kimura and Hakataya ran to the window to look outside, the drone of airplane engines had come directly overhead. Someone cried,

"Bomb!" We all instinctively crouched to take cover, and almost simultaneously a brilliant flash of light struck my eyes. Then there was a deep rumbling sound, followed the next instant by some tremendous force that brought the wall crashing down on top of us from behind. The room filled with bluish-yellow smoke. Wanting to confirm the safety of the others, I tried to stand up, but my right ear was ringing and I could not move freely. After a while I could hear cries of "help" "help" coming from left and right. The two nurses who had fallen beside me abruptly jumped to their feet. Kajiyama had a contusion on the back of her head, and both of them were covered in lime. I was apparently uninjured. The young man whom I had been treating was lying, unmoving, with his legs pinned between the wall and the medicine cabinet.

Outdoors it was dark and murky. The brown and yellow smoke was lifting gradually. The soil of the vegetable fields across the way was smoldering. We left the room and began to run through the hospital, trying desperately to assist the patients unable to move. We ran barefoot through the broken buildings and across the burning fields.

The sky was dark and the earth was red. Naked men, bloodied laborers, and women with disheveled hair ran wildly back and forth. No one had any clear destination; they just wanted to get away from where they were as quickly as possible. No one had any idea what had happened.

Since I had suffered not as much as a scratch, I decided to do whatever I could to help others. Although burning with a sense of purpose, I was also in a state of severe confusion. "Is there anyone uninjured?" I cried as loud as I could, and a young inpatient named Matsuo answered. There were three severely ill patients on the third floor, all young women. I called out to Brother Iwanaga, but at this point he was in the grove at the rear of the main building trying to free a nurse named Yamano from under fallen trees. I had no choice but to go upstairs and to carry the three patients out of the building one by one. The nurse, Ms. Murai, was a frail young woman but helped me as best she could.

I was concerned about the fate of Ms. Fukahori, our head nurse, but found to my great relief that she had survived with only minor injuries. However, Dr. Yoshioka, who had been upstairs at the time of the explosion, had suffered severe cuts to his face as a result of glass splinters. I was overcome with a dark premonition when I heard that Ms. Fukahori had applied first aid to these wounds and that Brother Iwanaga had carried the doctor to a refuge on the other side of the stream.

Fearing that Dr. Yoshioka had been mortally wounded, I left the hospital to see him, planning on cutting across the adjacent yard. But a middle-aged man grabbed me by the arm and stopped me. There was an injured boy of about six years old lying nearby, and the man begged me to help him. I did not have as much as a scrap of bandage with me, and so I could do nothing. I removed my arm from the grasp of the unfortunate man and ran to the spot where Dr. Yoshioka was lying. People with burns were lying in the water of the nearby stream. In the trees on the hillside I found Mr. Kinoshita, a teacher at Yamazato Primary School, lying in great pain with burns all over his body. Dr. Yoshioka was resting beside him.

Kawano, a student at Nagasaki Medical College, came along carrying an infant of about two years old who had suffered burns. I felt extremely encouraged to have this strong assistant. For about a month after that, Kawano made selfless contributions to the work of our hospital.

There was a beautiful chapel on the first floor of St. Francis Hospital, and a statue of Mary was enshrined there along with the Holy Eucharist. A student nurse named Matsuzaki, who had been working frantically to remove the patients from the hospital, suddenly remembered this and cried, "the Holy Eucharist!" I was also shocked by the realization. But fortunately Brother Iwanaga had already transferred the tabernacle and statue to the base of a pine tree on the hillside.

The three-story hospital was now enveloped in flames. The oil tank in the x-ray room was belching black smoke. The three best x-ray machines in Nagasaki, which had been evacuated here from Takahara Hospital only a week earlier, were now lost in the smoke and fire. A divinity student named Noguchi suggested that there was still time to go into the room and to remove some of the equipment, but when I looked at all the people dying around me I lost all desire to save a few machines. By four o'clock the hospital had been almost completely consumed by fire. A boy of about five years old lay dead beside the brick wall at the hospital entrance.

Urakami Cathedral, the largest church in the Far East, was sending clouds of black smoke to the sky. The Mitsubishi Arms Factory, which produced the torpedoes used in kamikaze attacks, was also burning, its exposed iron framing twisted like strands of taffy.

All of the Catholic facilities in the neighborhood – the orphanage known as the "Children's Room," the dormitory for women, the mission schools Junshin Jogakko and Josei Jogakko – were also enveloped in flames.

It was not until the nurse Ms. Murai asked me about my mother that I began to worry about my own family. My house was located on the western-side of the hospital where the blast generated by the atomic bomb explosion was felt the strongest. It had caught fire almost immediately, but my mother miraculously escaped without as much as a scratch. She had been out in the fields picking weeds when she heard the sound of airplanes and had immediately fled into a nearby air-raid shelter where she hid and prayed with her eyes closed. She did not even know that, outside, everything had been reduced to rubble and consumed by fire or that tens of thousands of lives had been cut short.

The clouded sky began to clear from the area over Motohara-machi. It was still daylight, but more than a month seemed to have passed since I woke up that morning. A thousand bags of brown rice and other foods such as miso and soy sauce had been stored in the hospital warehouse for use in emergencies. Thus we were able to build a fireplace with broken bricks in the middle of the yard and to begin cooking rice for the injured. The wounded grasped the rice balls with blackened fingers and carried them to their mouths.

If I had not been a physician, I might not have felt such a huge burden of responsibility. I would have been able to rejoice with others over our survival. Perhaps I would have fled to some safe place.　But I am a physician.　I could not turn away when there were people with terrible burns and injuries lying in the yard moaning for help.　The hospital buildings were destroyed and all of the medical supplies and equipment consumed by fire, but as long as there were patients, it was my duty as a physician to look after them.

The sun finally set.　I had to begin by finding shelter for Mr. Kinoshita and Dr. Yoshioka, who were lying on the hillside across the stream.　The former was so severely burned that his facial features were indiscernible.　His young wife was at his side, applying ointment to the burns.　From time to time he cried out in pain, but there was nothing that I could do to alleviate his suffering.　Kawano took him up on his back and, with Ms. Kinoshita and I walking silently behind, carried him down the cluttered path to the warehouse where we put him down to rest on a bed of straw mats.

Dr. Yoshioka's mother and older brother had come in search of him.　He had lost a lot of blood and so frequently lost consciousness, making me worry that he was about to take his last breath.

The head nurse, Ms. Murakami, was injured and exhausted from all her hard work, but she continued to labor selflessly – perhaps out of a sense of mission as a nurse – and to attend to the burns of the infant brought in earlier by Kawano.　The child cried hysterically for his mother, making it very difficult for the head nurse.　A woman was probably sitting, somewhere in the ruins, crying out this child's name throughout the night.

The night grew late.　The wild, agonized voices of people calling out the names of children, mothers and husbands echoed here and there, the sounds cutting to the depths of our hearts.

The hospital was still burning.　Trying desperately to at least save the food cellar, Brother Iwanaga was carrying water in tubs on a balancing pole and splashing this through the windows with a long-handled fertilizer dipper.　He must have carried several hundred tubs of water that night.　I watched him with tears in my eyes.

People with burns and injuries came to the hospital in an unending procession.　When they realized that the hospital had been destroyed as well, many mustered up courage and continued along the path over the mountain, but 50 or 60 lost all desire to go on and collapsed in the yard.   It was unbearable for me to have these people right in front of me but to be able to do nothing to help them.

That night, I was not the only one unable to catch a wink of sleep.   Everyone in Nagasaki seemed to be searching for someone.

"Tanaka Heikichi of Matsuyama-machi!"

"Is Fujimura Toshiko of the Municipal Girls School here?"

These loud voices sometimes elicited responses, but the majority just echoed emptily in the darkness.   The people being called were probably all dead.   Or perhaps some were lying on the verge of death in the forests above the city.   In any case, thousands – no, tens of thousands – of people fled that night over the hillsides of Nishiyama and Mt. Kompira.   I wonder how far they got?   The injured piled upon the injured, and corpses piled up one upon the other, filling the night sky with a ghostly sadness and tainting the air with the smell of wasted blood.

August 10

Urakami Cathedral and the Mitsubishi Arms Factory were still burning.   Not a single person seemed to remain in the Motohara-machi neighborhood.   Was everyone dead?

Noguchi led me to the charcoal cellar in the hospital basement, where we found two large boxes that Noguchi had dragged out. Opening the lids, I found that these contained gauze, cotton batting, bandages and other medical supplies and drugs.   It was like meeting the Buddha in hell.   I embraced Noguchi in a fit of joy.   The quantity was far from sufficient, but still it would allow me to fulfill my duties to small some degree at least.

If there has been one moment in my life when I accomplished the physician's humanitarian ideal, then it was certainly this day at this time.   I began by administering an antibiotic solution to Mr. Kinoshita's burns and covering these with sterile gauze.   I did not stop to consider whether or not this would prove helpful in the treatment of burns.   Kinoshita looked up at me while I worked, asking me, "Will I make it?" over and over again.   I had no alternative of course but to say, "Yes, you're going to be fine."

Airplanes were constantly flying over the city, giving the air-raid sirens no rest. The inpatients were lying, without mats or cover, on the earthen floor of the rice warehouse. They called my name from left and right, begging for help. Everyone considered his or her own injury to be of foremost importance and had no time to think of others.

There had been something bothering me from the previous day, a worry that I could not bring up. That was the fate of the parents of head nurse Fukahori. Her mother lived just behind Urakami Cathedral, and her brother and sister-in-law had both been working at the arms factory near the hypocenter. We had all been aware of this but had been unable to say anything in this chaotic situation.

Noguchi intuited my concerns and went out to gather information, but his reports only confirmed our worst fears. It was an ordeal just to look at Ms. Fukahori. All I could do was pray silently that, through the mercy of Mary, she would somehow be able to endure this terrible grief.

The streets of Motohara-machi were deserted. It was a city of death. The only thing still functioning seemed to be our St. Francis Hospital. We boiled slices of squash, cooked rice and made rice balls for the hundreds of people who gathered in the hospital yard. All of the people who assisted in these activities had lost their homes and had family members dead or injured, but they dismissed their own sorrow and showed the first signs of Nagasaki's recovery from this calamity.

I heard that Mr. Kinoshita had been carried to an air-raid shelter and went to check on him, only to find that his breath was weak and his pupils widely dilated. Death was obviously approaching. The people around him begged me to do something, but there was nothing left except prayer: "Jesus, Mary and Joseph please pray for us." I left the air-raid shelter with the sounds of this invocation lingering in my ears. Kinoshita's wife came out with me, carrying a baby on her back, and asked me, not with words but with her worrying eyes, how I thought her husband would fare. "There is no hope," I answered, also using only my eyes. We stood there in silence for a few seconds.   Then she broke down and began to weep in a loud voice.

The sun set soon after I returned to the hospital.   Flames were still darting up from the ruins of Nagasaki.   I joined Kawano, Murai and the others in curling up with blankets in a corner of the hospital yard.   In a nearby field, within earshot from my pillow, a cow that had fled from somewhere emitted forlorn wails of "moo" "moo" all through the night.

August 11

Brother Shirahama, who had been unconscious since the atomic bomb explosion, seemed to be doing better today.   Fr. Ishikawa's facial wound, suffered when he was thrown against the wall, had swollen a little, and he was groaning with pain in the air-raid shelter.   The corpse of an elderly man was lying in the potato field in front of the hospital.   He had suffered burns all over his body and probably died the night before.   It was impossible to determine his identity.   The child carried in by Kawano had cried all night for a drink of water from his mother and then died at dawn.

Family members of the injured brought several large bamboo poles.   Using these as pillars and draping straw mats over the sides, we erected a makeshift relief station where Kawano and I took responsibility for medical treatment.   Ms. Murai and the other nurses meanwhile worked with superhuman energy, cooking meals and attending to the wounded.

Someone told me that Ms. Yamano, the nurse who had been pinned under a tree, was suffering terribly in the air-raid shelter, and so I went to see her.   She complained of severe dizziness and nausea. I attributed her symptoms to the cramped conditions in the shelter, but in retrospect it is safe to say that these were late effects of exposure to atomic bomb radiation.

Many of the people visiting the relief station now were suffering, not from burns, but from severe inflammation of the oral mucosa, swelling around the mouth, and bloody stools.   They followed the same course from inflammation of the mouth to swelling of the gums, bloody stools, nausea and, finally, death.

Kawano came along with two pieces of happy news. Both my father and the mother of head nurse Fukahori had escaped injury.

People who had suffered burns but were otherwise in good health began to arrive at our hospital in increasing numbers. We felt enormously relieved to see these people, because they seemed to signify an end to the injuries caused by the atomic bombing. But we were utterly ignorant of the true effects of the atomic bomb. Heat had not been the only form of energy generated by the blast. Another invisible but deadly force had been unleashed, digging deep into the earth, penetrating to the very marrow of the victims' bones, and destroying living cells. We had no idea at all about this. We reveled in short-lived joy at having been shielded by buildings and thus spared burns, but we soon learned that the grim reality of science allowed no easy miracles.

After the sun went down we all sprawled out on the grass. Dr. Takahara's voice sounded in the distance. We all got up and greeted him happily. He apologized over and over again for being so late in coming. We, on the other hand, expressed regret that his x-ray equipment had been destroyed. He spoke with tears running down his cheeks about the terrible carnage that he had witnessed along the way. We sat around him, listening silently. We were really in a complete fog about the horrors of modern warfare. Indeed, we were involved in a war that none of us could even understand.

August 12

Dr. Takahara left early that morning, and I had to commence treatment once again. A teacher at Shiroyama Primary School, a woman of about 20 years old, came to the hospital on unsteady legs. Exposed to the explosion during a staff meeting, she had suffered cuts from glass splinters all over her body and, unable to return home or to make any progress through the terrible heat in the ruins, she had spent two days in the water of a river before finally finding her way here.

When I examined her I found that more than 100 glass splinters of various sizes were lodged in her skin. It was amazing that she had survived. Kawano and I worked for an hour to remove the splinters but could still not finish the job, and the young woman cried in pain again and again throughout the procedure.

By around two o'clock, more than 200 patients had been carried to our temporary facility. I had to treat these people single-handedly. Most of them were unknown to me, and all had suffered life-threatening injuries. I walked amidst the rows of patients, spreading zinc ointment on burns and applying disinfected gauzes to wounds. Even after sunset, my hands continued to work like machines under the light of candles.

Suddenly, the sound of an airplane echoed in the distance. "Blow out the candles!" "Flee to the air-raid shelter!" "Mother, mother!" "Help!" The darkness filled with cries of terror. After the sound of the airplane passed, we crawled out of the shelter, relit the candles and continued our work.

At eleven o'clock I finally threw down my tweezers. Untreated patients were calling me, but my fingers were now as stiff as stone. The head nurse and Ms. Murai rubbed my hands and legs and tried to comfort me.

August 13

When I awoke, thoughts of all the work that faced me weighed down heavily on my heart and I could not find the strength to get up. It made me bitterly sad to be a doctor, but the medical student, Kawano, and the young nurses inspired me with their shining example of courage. They were just as exhausted as me, if not even more exhausted, but they rose early to prepare the treatment room for me.

Because of my nervous character, I sometimes screamed at patients, even the seriously injured. But Kawano, who was a devout Catholic, intermediated each time with a spirit of generosity and endurance. I began another day's work, my crumbling sense of purpose bolstered by the goodwill of these people.

The nurses were extremely busy, not only assisting me but also attending to the preparation of meals. They boiled brown rice in a pot under the hot sun, then pressed handfuls of the rice into balls and distributed two of these to each patient. Slices of cooked squash served as a side dish. They prepared this meal three times a day for 200 people, no easy task. Some of them had suffered injuries themselves. They had lost their homes. Some of their relatives were dead or missing, while others had suffered serious injuries. Yet still they stayed heroically at their respective posts. I wondered if the members of the air defense forces, who before had put up such a strong front, were showing this level of bravery. What were the members of the "patriotic women's corps" doing? They were probably all absorbed exclusively in their own problems, utterly oblivious to the sufferings of their neighbors. In the nurses laboring alongside me I saw the strength and beauty of women living in faith.

I had been delighted to hear that the mother of Ms. Fukahori, the head nurse, had escaped injury, but we received notice today that she had fallen into a critical condition. Noguchi (the divinity student) and Brother Iwanaga went out and carried her back to the hospital. She was a robust woman of about 70 years old. We placed her beside the concrete bathhouse and I examined her there, but her complexion was purple in color and she was breathing erratically. Ms. Fukahori came to her side and called her name, but it was all to no avail. Ms. Fukahori could only embrace her mother in an agony of grief. For 70 years this good woman had offered herself to Mary and devoted her time to others, but now her life of mercy had to end in this grim place, under these terrible circumstances.

August 14

It was another hot sultry day. The previously silent Motohara-machi neighborhood finally began to show signs of activity. Also, flies and mosquitoes, which had been nonexistent since the bombing, returned and multiplied with astonishing vitality. At the same time an indescribable stench filled the air. The people who had escaped from instant death had celebrated their victory over the atomic bomb, but now a fearsome wave of infection and deterioration was sweeping over the wasteland. More and more people became blackish-blue in the face, lost their hair in one night, bled from the nose and mouth and suffered bloody diarrhea. A dark shadow of death was creeping over the entire district.

The people of Urakami were accustomed to hardships, and they had been taught from birth to revel in sacrifice. But the present ordeal was more serious than anyone could imagine. People who thought they had miraculously escaped injury began to die one after another from radiation sickness, a scourge of terror that lasted for more than 20 days.

August 15

For Catholics, August 15 was the holy day of the Ascension. I was treating outpatients at the hospital gate when a woman from the neighborhood came along and reported that Japan had announced its unconditional surrender. This news did not surprise me at all. Then two policemen appeared, denounced the news of surrender as a groundless rumor, and led the woman off somewhere for interrogation.

Around noon an aircraft embellished with the Union Jack flew low over the city, making everyone dive to the floor or flee for cover.

The sun went down and darkness set in. Kawano, who had gone out earlier to look for medical supplies, came back and reported that the rumor of surrender had indeed been true. According to someone who had been listening to the radio in Isahaya, the Emperor himself had made the announcement. When Kawano read a transcript of the announcement aloud, the nurses could no longer stand and collapsed onto the grass, sobbing. The military police had tried to ban the broadcast of this announcement in Nagasaki, and they put up posters on telephone poles calling the surrender a lie and insisting that Japan would continue fighting on the home islands if necessary.

This useless pawing on the part of the military police filled me with rage. People who had no grasp of the devastation caused by the atomic bombing might lament Japan's surrender, but for people like us who had experienced it first-hand, there was no surprise whatever in the fact that the Emperor had taken this step.

The war was over. Now what were we to do, stranded in the atomic wasteland? No one had any answer. The only reality was that we had to drum up strength and continue – today, tomorrow and the next day – to treat the countless people in front of us suffering from atomic bomb injuries. As silent as stone statues, we just sat there nibbling at cold squash and crumbly rice balls and watching the candle flames flicker wildly in the breeze.

The above is a record of my experiences from August 9, 1945, the day that an atomic bomb exploded over Nagasaki, until August 15 when Japan announced its unconditional surrender. It is a story of the human love that unfolded at the devastated No.1 Urakami Hospital (present-day St. Francis Hospital), where doctors, nurses and Catholic brothers worked selflessly for the victims in the ruined city. A Canadian Franciscan priest who read it commented as follows: "I hope for the perfect success of this account. And I pray that the world will be better, more peaceful, and never again encounter another week of horror like this."

(The author, Akizuki Tatsuichiro, graduated from Kyoto University School of Medicine and began work at both Nagasaki Medical College and the Takahara Hospital in downtown Nagasaki. In September 1944 he was appointed director of St. Francis Hospital in Urakami Motohara-machi and devoted himself to the treatment of more than 60 tuberculosis patients. He worked alongside Catholic priests, brothers and nurses, and courageously maintained his hospital in the midst of the atomic bomb tragedy.)

Excerpt from "The Earth Was Stripped Naked"

From Memories of Darkness and Hardship: Up Until the Day Shiroyama Primary School Was Closed

Chiyoko Egashira

The ruins of Shiroyama Primary School (500 meters from the hypocenter). Bodies of the victims were cremated in the area in the forefront.

A "new-type bomb" exploded over Hiroshima on August 6, 1945. Only hours later, President Truman released the following statement to the world: "The Japanese began the war from the air at Pearl Harbor. They have been repaid many fold. And the end is not yet. With this bomb we have now added a new and revolutionary increase in destruction to supplement the growing power of our armed forces. In their present form these bombs are now in production and even more powerful forms are in development. It is an atomic bomb. It is a harnessing of the basic power of the universe."

We did not hear this statement in Japan. Two days later on August 8, the entire staff of Shiroyama Primary School was scheduled to go to pick weeds in the school's rice paddies in Nagayo Village, on the other side of the Urakami Reservoir. Over breakfast, I spoke with my husband about the short article in the morning newspaper reporting the explosion of a new-type bomb over Hiroshima.

"Perhaps we should evacuate grandmother and the children to the countryside," said my husband, speaking in an unusually serious tone. The Shiroyama neighborhood had not experienced an air raid to date. On the contrary, people were coming to Shiroyama as part of the evacuation of downtown neighborhoods, and the number of households was much higher than that prior to the war. In fact I felt quite safe, living in the Shiroyama neighborhood where there was not a single factory. As I did every morning, I watched as my children put on their matching *monpe* (baggy cotton trousers) and took up their rucksacks, and I went with them to the neighborhood air-raid shelter. Then I hurried off, planning to reach the meeting place at Oide in Urakami by nine o'clock and hoping that there would be no air-raid alarm.

Along the way I fell in with Shizuko Nagata, one of my fellow teachers. "It seems that a new-type bomb fell on Hiroshima, but there is no reason in this rural area to make the children stay in the air-raid shelters," laughed Shizuko as we made our way to our destination. "The next time, let's give them all a ride in the pull carts."

Before our school principal arrived, we visited the farmhouses nearby to purchase squashes and potatoes for our lunch that day.

While we were doing that, Ms. Murakami, one of our new teachers, came along wiping tears from her eyes. It seemed that an alarm had been sounded and she had been forced into an air-raid shelter by members of her local civilian defense force, and that, despite this unavoidable circumstance, she had been severely scolded by the principal for being late.

This was our second time to pull weeds in the rice paddies. The paddy on the hillside was fed by spring water and painfully cold, yet the paddy in the sunny lower area was unpleasantly warm and slimy. As if to add to this discomfort, the sharp leaves of the rice plants jabbed our faces and hands and made them swell. But everyone worked hard, and the squash porridge we ate after this backbreaking work was delicious.

After lunch, sitting on the ledge between the rice paddies, Ms. Kurihara (one of the teachers in the same grade) and I joined in singing "Lorelei" It was our first time to sing together in ages. A beautiful woman with a lovely voice, Ms. Kurihara was the sixth-grade homeroom teacher of my daughter Mitsuko.

"Today we have finished enough work for two days," announced our principal. "So let's gather at school tomorrow at nine o'clock." After that we broke up to go home. (If we had stretched the weed-pulling out over two days, we would all have escaped from the atomic bombing.)

On the way home I encountered a sudden shower and got wet to the skin. By the time I got home it was already dark.

August 9

The sky was overcast, and the air was humid. An air-raid alert was sounded early in the morning, and so we finished breakfast hastily for fear another warning might be sounded. While I was filling my children's emergency bags with food and first-aid supplies, a task that by now had become a daily routine, my eldest daughter told me that her sister Harumi had been chewing on tissue paper in the air-raid shelter. I looked in Harumi's bag and found that some honey had leaked into a bunch of tissues, creating sweet wafer-like sheets. This and other simple snacks, like the donuts I made from rationed flour, were the children's only pleasure in the air-raid shelter.

My eldest son Takashi, winding gaiters around his legs, asked with a smile, "Mom, can I go fishing with Dad at Teguma?"

Just then, the radio announced that an air-raid alert had been sounded at 7:40 a.m., and a tense atmosphere gripped my family. My husband hurried my mother and four daughters off into the neighborhood air-raid shelter, and then came back for a tatami mat and carried it into the shelter.

After returning from the shelter he told me that he had made a bed for our daughter Naomi. Just then, another voice came over the radio, announcing that a more urgent "air-raid warning" had been sounded at 7:50 a.m. for the Nagasaki District. Civilian air-raid wardens shouted the same warning as they walked around the neighborhood. Terrified, I crouched in the air-raid shelter dug under the floor of the house. My husband, who soon rushed into the shelter, also had a grave expression on his face.

After a while, however, we heard with relief the announcement that an "all clear" had been declared at 8:30 a.m.

Even in mid-summer women had to wear baggy dark-colored cotton trousers. I had made these trousers from a formal kimono that I had worn in my primary school days and that had an auspicious pine-bamboo-plum pattern dyed on its long sleeves. My three daughters, wearing the trousers made by their mother, came home from the shelter romping about with rucksacks on their backs, as if they had returned from playing with their friends. Everyday, Harumi, aged six, and four year-old Kazumi went to the shelter with picture books, dolls and woven *temari* handballs, led by the hand by my eldest daughter Mitsuko.

My husband and eldest son both left for work. My son, a student at Keiho Middle School in Takenokubo-machi, had been mobilized to work at the Nittsu Nagasaki branch office as a member of the naval foodstuffs transport team. My husband was a leader of the students from Nagasaki Commercial School mobilized to work in the arms factory. Little did we know that we were bidding each other an eternal farewell.

My mother, who had taken shelter with the children, returned home with my youngest daughter Naomi (one year and two months old), saying, "Naomi burst out crying immediately after getting into the air-raid shelter and she would not stop crying however hard I tried to console her." Both were wet all over with perspiration. Later I departed for Shiroyama Primary School with Naomi strapped to my back. It was my first time to take her to school this way.

Now devoid of pupils, the classrooms were silent and vacant. Compared to the air-raid shelter, this was a much more comfortable place of refuge. After the morning ceremony, the staff separated into two groups and set to work near the front gate and the back gate respectively, leaving Principal Shimizu, Vice-principal Arakawa, Mr. Kogawara, Mr. Kinoshita, Mr. Shimamura and five women teachers. Three male teachers, Mr. Banto, Mr. Nakamura and Mr. Miyamoto, were on duty as lookouts on the rooftop and other places around the school.

The work allotted to the women was to carry worn-out tatami mats to the schoolyard for evacuation purposes. We did the work in pairs, chatting on topics such as the weeding we had done in the paddy fields in Nagayo Village the day before or recent articles in the newspapers. While I engaged in this work, my baby Naomi was moving her hands and feet cheerfully, cackling joyfully each time I bent over or straightened up. After arranging about fifty mats in the playground, we began to weed and clean the backyard of the school without noticing the time passing.

The central part of the playground, inside the track around which pupils ran races, had been plowed for cultivation of sweet potatoes, forming an oval shape. The leaves of the potato plants formed a lush green carpet, and the noisy chirping of cicadas echoed from the hillside behind the school compound. The second and third-floor classrooms on the south side of the school were being used as workshops for about 200 students mobilized as Mitsubishi factory workers. The girls could be seen working in twos and threes through the windows, but otherwise the school was calm and quiet. At a meeting in the principal's office, we agreed that, because of the increasing frequency of air-raid warnings, the women should share in night duty in order to lighten the heavy burden presently carried by the male teachers.

By now very few victory parades were being conducted. It was clear that the tide of war had turned against Japan, and although we put on a brave face, we were all filled inwardly with apprehension. Mieko Matsunaga, a server in the kitchen, told me that she was going up to the roof to collect the potato strips drying in the sun, and she kindly offered to take Naomi with her. Seeing Naomi smiling happily on my back, I declined her offer and continued my work, urging her to finish her allotted tasks as quickly as possible.

All the while, an air-raid alert had been in effect. Around 11 o'clock, Ms. Takahashi, still holding a broom in her hands, told me that Naomi was asleep on my back. I walked quietly behind the principal's office and entered the nurse's room, intending to put Naomi to bed. There were two beds in the room, one of them by the window. The other had been fashioned with two tatami mats, on top of which was piled a new futon set that had been donated for teachers on night duty by the Women's Patriotic League. The atomic bomb exploded just when I reached for the straps on my back in order to untie Naomi and lay her down in the shadow of the futon.

In the midst of that deafening roar, my first thought was that an enemy bomber had crashed through the windows and exploded right over my head. Along with the tremendous sound, I felt a sharp pain as if my body were being torn in two. All at once I threw myself over my baby to protect her.

The atomic bomb that fell into a corner of the Urakami neighborhood,
like a thread of cloud descending from the sky,
exploded over my head at Shiroyama Primary School,
only 450 meters from the hypocenter.
It exploded over the heads of my children playing house
and my elderly mother in our home.
It exploded over the head of my son,
a mobilized student helping to transport foodstuffs.
It exploded over the head of my husband,

working as a leader of mobilized students.
It exploded over the roof of my parents' house,
located three kilometers away.
It exploded over the heads of my pupils,
dreaming with their families of a happy future.
It exploded over the heads of tens of thousands of Nagasaki citizens.

That morbid roar, like a subterranean rumble.
That cloud of dust and debris that rushed wildly through the air,
masking the light of the sun and erasing the lines of the earth.
One instant!!
Oh, just one instant!!
The dust turned to flames,
a conflagration churning up into the sky,
roaring with devilish power through the city,
transforming the city of the cross, the city of peace,
into a living hell of fire.

The school buildings collapsed and the air filled with brownish-yellow dust like a smoke screen. I could even hear the ground rumbling. So stricken with fear and panic that my hair stood on end, I embraced my baby – who now looked like a demon smeared with blood – and crawled out frantically from the nurse's room.

Drug shelves, windowpanes and everything else were smashed to pieces. I could see electric wires burning in the distance through the broken wall of the principal's office. The voice of a woman echoed faintly from the principal's office, crying "Help! Please help me!" I could also see Vice-principal Arakawa standing on a collapsed bureau. Mr. Kogawara was lying dead, his hands grasping the edge of the principal's coat so tightly that his skin seemed embedded in the cloth.

Naomi was unable even to cry, and I was so overcome with terror that I could not find the strength to cry for help. Blood had spattered from my wounds onto Naomi's face. Her hair was frizzled and erect. Her whole body, except her eyes and mouth, was smeared with ashes. She appeared non-human, almost demonic. Her inability to cry made me fear that she was dead.

I looked down on the Shiroyama neighborhood through the broken windows in the hall adjoining the nurse's room. Not a single house was left standing. There was nothing left except clouds of dust. Overcome with apprehension, I decided to leave the school by the front gate and try to find my way home.

I found the big gateposts lying on their side with the mud-covered bases ripped from the ground like teeth pulled out of their gums. The old Japanese bead tree measuring several arm spans, cherry trees, cedars, the janitor's room, the night-duty room – everything that once existed here had been blown away and smashed to pieces. There was hardly room enough to step. I saw the janitor walking up the stone pavement like a sleepwalker. In the face of all these terrible scenes, I lost my desire to go home and decided to return to the place where I had been before.

The demolished houses in the Shiroyama residential neighborhood, which before had been hidden under clouds of dust, were now enveloped in a sea of flames the spread endlessly and scorched the sky red. I sat down at the foot of the staircase, holding my baby who looked like a living corpse. Vice-principal Arakawa came by from the direction of the front gate, helping along two unidentifiable women. I wanted to call him, but my voice was frozen with horror.

I do not know how much time passed. After a while I heard my husband's voice calling me from somewhere: "Egashira! Egashira!" At first I thought I was dreaming, but the sound came nearer. I tried to call out his name but I had no voice to emit or tears to shed. When he finally found me, I could only cling to him fiercely and silently. My shoes had come off in the commotion, and my feet were bleeding.

My husband picked up Naomi and led his wounded wife out of the buildings and into the schoolyard. The sweet potato plants that had been growing here thick and green were gone, leaving behind only singed reddish-brown soil. Not as much as a blade of grass remained. The air raid shelter built on the west side of the schoolyard was crowded with injured people. Some were lying at the entrance with their internal organs hanging out.

"We will only die here," we said to each other as we left the shelter, climbing the hillside fields now naked except for a few scorched pumpkins scattered about. I heard someone speak in my direction, offering encouraging words, but we trudged up the hillside with the other people.

One person after another fell dead along the way, crying "Help me mother! Please help me!" or "Water! Please give me water!" The boy walking ahead of us also collapsed shouting, "The Emperor forever! Mother! Mother!"

Cries for water echoed all around us. The next thing I knew I was lying in a shelter near Tateiwa Shinto Shrine. I had apparently lost consciousness along the way and had to be carried there.

The mushroom cloud had been streaked with beautiful colors, but a living hell on earth had unfolded under it, a fearsome hell in which humanity annihilates fellow humanity. The living dead wandered, with burned flesh hanging off their limbs, through the atomic firestorm. Our family was just one among thousands.

I had bent over instinctively to protect my baby at the moment of the atomic bomb explosion. As a result, my back was covered with glass shards and splinters of wood like a pincushion. I lay face downward in the shelter, unable to move. Both Naomi and I became nauseous and vomited constantly, finally throwing up a yellow fluid. We could not even take a drink of water.

The sun was concealed behind a veil of dust, its rays so dim that it was difficult to tell when daytime turned into night. Trees made a morbid crackling sound as they burned on nearby hillsides. Interspersed among these sounds were the voices of the people who came in and out of the shelter searching for loved ones. I heard a mother holding her baby and crying, "Don't die! Oh please don't die!" But soon the sound was no more.

After carrying Naomi and me into this tiny cave-like shelter, my husband went out to see what had become of our house, but the fires were still raging and he could not get close to it. He had no choice but to come back to the shelter and wait for the fires to die down.

The glow of the fires consuming the city and hillsides was so bright that dawn came all but unnoticed. I heard the roar of an airplane flying low overhead several times during the night, and I lay face downward worried sick about my children and mother somewhere out there in the ruins.

"Mrs. Egashira! Mrs. Egashira! Where is Mitsuko?" Someone came over to the spot where I was lying, and I realized that it was Ritsuko, a friend of my daughter Mitsuko and one of my former pupils. It seemed that her uncle managed the air-raid shelter. Her house, although spared from fire, had been completely demolished. "My father and other relatives were killed," sobbed Ritsuko, holding Naomi in her arms like her own sister.

My husband had been exposed to the explosion while conferring with colleagues about the mobilization of students to work at the Mitsubishi Arms Factory in Urakami. He had rescued me from the ruins, comforting me and urging me not to worry because he had escaped uninjured. I had also managed to survive, but my heart wanted to burst when I thought about my mother and three daughters who perhaps died searching in vain for us.

When the heat relented, my husband was finally able to approach the ruins of our house. After a while he returned with the ashes of my mother and three daughters in a pot he had found amid the debris.

"You can't lose heart, Chiyoko," said my husband without looking at me, his eyes swollen with tears. The image of my children and mother when we parted on the morning of August 9 came to mind, and I felt as if I heard them calling me.

I could not find any more tears to shed over the clumps of white ash that were my children and mother. I could only embrace the broken pot, crying, "Forgive your mother, please. Why couldn't I die with you? Please, please forgive me."

"Takashi suffered severe burns," reported my husband. "He is lying in the shelter in our neighborhood. He managed to make his way home from his office and then was carried to the shelter. Harumi was found by Mr. Takeda, who had been searching for his own wife and children. She was lying burned and dead in front of the Takeda family house. He identified her by the name on her jacket badge." How heartbreaking and unendurable it must have been for my husband to cremate his daughters and collect their ashes!

"The Shiroyama area is a sea of fire. To get near the residential area I had to take a detour from Hachiman Shrine to Gokoku Shrine. The flames are still raging and it's scorching hot... A woman who had been carrying a dead child in her arms suddenly threw the corpse onto the roadside, as if she had gone mad... Horses were lying dead in large numbers, their bodies burned and swollen... The men working at Mitsubishi and the prefectural and municipal government offices were searching desperately for family members, and dumbfounded by the destruction... Urakami River is filled with the corpses of people who rushed there trying to escape the heat..."

My husband's words seemed to catch my ears only in disconnected spurts.

I learned later that rescue teams came several times to a spot below our shelter to distribute rice balls and relief goods to the sufferers, but unfortunately these did not reach us. Shortly after noon on August 11, just when I was looking at a cloud that looked like a sleeping child and thinking it was trying to tell me something, my brother from Suwa-machi and my older sister and her husband came looking for us.

"I came back to Nagasaki yesterday," reported my brother. "I heard that the Shiroyama neighborhood had been completely destroyed, and I assumed that the whole Egashira famly had been killed. I went into the burned out area this morning and found Takashi in the shelter, and he told me that you were here. I was astonished. I went home again to get a stretcher. It's wonderful that you have survived!" The fires spread as far as the prefecture government office and the Sakaya-machi neighborhood, but Suwa-machi was saved because it's on the other side of Nakashima River."

My brother-in-law also reported his experiences: "It was as though a bomb had exploded right over the roof of our house, but no one was injured. I was watching my son play chess on the veranda. We were blown into the interior of the house. People in the neighborhood started saying that another bomb would soon be dropped on the prefecture government office. Everyone fled, leaving all the windows and doors on the houses open. We spent two nights in a mausoleum under a family grave."

My brother and brother-in-law lifted me onto a stretcher, and I listened to their stories while being carried down the streets.

I begged them to carry me to my house. I wanted to apologize to my deceased children, pressing my palms together in prayer. The areas that we passed were so devastated that it was hard even to make out the lines of familiar streets. The gray, lifeless ruins stretched away endlessly. It is no wonder people concluded that plants would not grow here for 75 years to come.

We reached the shelter where my son Takashi was lying. His entire body was bandaged, leaving spaces only for his eyes and mouth. "Mother!" I recognized the voice of my son. Having lost the energy even to try to console him, I just took hold of his cold hands and squeezed them with a feeling of grief and bewilderment.

After that Takashi and I were carried together to a temporary relief station set up on the site of the Mitsubishi Arms Factory. We just lay numb as we rocked along on the stretchers, crossing Ohashi Bridge through the stench of burning corpses.

The scenes of horror and misery were so shocking that one wanted to turn away: a streetcar driver burned black but still grasping the steering lever, dead horses charred like gleaming coal, twisted streetcar tracks lurching up from the ground like strands of taffy, and rows of large cherry trees ripped up by the roots.

The temporary relief station at the arms factory in Urakami was a dark place with rough straw mats spread out directly on the ground. Hundreds of victims were lying naked on the straw mats, all in such a ghastly state that it was hard to distinguish the living from the dead.

"Cut off the underwear," said the doctor to his assistant in a harsh tone of voice. They both looked exhausted. I was stripped of my underwear just as an animal is flayed. Broken glass fell away from the cloth. Then the doctor used tweezers to extract the splinters of glass and wood splinters sticking into my back. Lying face down on the rough straw mat, I did my best to endure the pain. My husband told me later that he counted the fragments one by one but passed out from exhaustion after reaching about 90.

"I removed the larger splinters," said the doctor, stopping the operation and sprinkling antiseptic over my back. "The small ones will probably come out on their own."

It filled me with sadness to think about Takashi, who was lying in the adjoining room and undoubtedly enduring pain much greater than mine.

Although part of Nagasaki City, Suwa-machi escaped destruction by the atomic bomb because of its distance from the hypocenter. Since my parents' home was located in that neighborhood, we considered the possibility of taking refuge there. But another air raid could come at any time, and so we decided instead to go to a house in a more remote area called Kawabira, where we had made arrangements for an evacuation place the previous year. We left at night, carrying lanterns and listening attentively for the sound of airplanes. We found our way from Oide to Kawabira, via an out of the way place called Tottomizuhira, and called at the house of a student from the commercial high school. It seemed that the student's aunt had left for town and was now missing, but despite the hectic situation, the family kindly allowed us to settle in the entrance lobby of their house. It was a great relief.

Takashi, still bandaged from head to toe, began to lose his appetite as his condition deteriorated and finally was unable even to drink water. Someone in the village kindly suggested that mulberry leaves are good for the treatment of burns, and so my husband searched for these leaves, toasted them over a fire and applied them to Takashi's burns. We used cold water from the stream but were still unable to bring his temperature down. We wanted to call a doctor, but no hospitals remained. Despite his critical condition, Takashi occasionally jumped to his feet. After that he lost all sense of night and day, and his calls to us grew weak. We were also at a complete loss to relieve the sufferings of our son.

The injured were dying one after another, and, knowing nothing about atomic bomb radiation, people began to call the disease a pestilence and to refuse to stay with sufferers under the same roof.

No longer welcome in our present accommodations, we borrowed a small room elsewhere and continued to attend to Takashi, but to our great sorrow, he died in his parents' arms on the fifth day after the atomic bombing.

Once again it fell upon my husband to wrap Takashi's dead body in a blanket and to carry him by cart to the site of our house in Shiroyama for cremation, the same spot where Takashi's grandmother and younger sisters had been cremated a few days earlier. Forgetting my pain and holding Naomi firmly in my arms, I saw the cart off, weeping and gnawing my lips until it disappeared from sight.

We started a new life there, making use of pots, knives, eating utensils and other things collected from the rubble. We used a foot-operated rice cleaner to polish the brown rice rationed at the time, and split firewood into small pieces and used it to cook the rice over a clay stove. Our drinking water came from a well on a neighbor's property 50 meters away, and we washed our clothes in the river. It was an inconvenient lifestyle to say the least.

My husband, claiming that he was uninjured and healthy, walked as much as 20 kilometers a day to deal with the aftermath at the commercial high school, and on his way back he carried our rationed items.

The injuries to my legs were so severe that I had to crawl about during the first days. There was no mirror and so I had no way to see my own appearance, but when I went to the river I was shocked to see my reflection in the river. Half of my face was purple and swollen, like a ghost returning from the dead. After Takashi's death, heavy rains continued for several days and seemed to wash away all the defilements in the wasteland. Water rose to the banks of the river, hiding the stepping-stones and destroying a wooden bridge.

After the atomic bombing, airplanes – on which side I could not tell – continued to fly over Nagasaki, and every time the sound of roaring engines reached their ears the people scrambled their belongings together and fled to the hillsides. Someone urged me to take refuge in an air-raid shelter, but I just looked up at the sky hoping that I would be able to follow my dead son as soon as possible.

August 15

On August 15, my next-door neighbor told me about the Emperor's radio message declaring the end of the war.

My son Takashi was supposed to have entered the Naval Academy just that day. He had been recommended to the academy by the school authorities of Keiho Middle School (the predecessor of the present-day Nishi Senior High School) because of his excellent grades. Call it a twist of fate, but for me the irony only made me throw my arms up in despair.

The following evening our neighbor's son suddenly returned from his Special Attack (Kamikaze) Unit. I can still vividly recall the sound of his aunt's voice when she grabbed him by the collar and screamed, "Why have you returned? Look at the horrors visited upon the Egashira family! It is because you went off, determined to die for your country, but now come shamelessly back that all of this has happened!"

"There is no cure for atomic disease."

"Once you get this disease, no medicine or treatment will help. All you can do is wait to die."

"The body begins to melt and maggots infest the wounds of the living."

"Not as much as a blade of grass will grow in the Urakami area for 75 years to come."

"Someone ate a pumpkin from the ruins and died from the ensuing diarrhea."

"The wells are all poisoned."

"Thieves are coming into the wasteland to steal watches and rings from the dead, and they're carrying their booty away by the cartload."

"No, I saw them using a horse-drawn cart."

Various groundless rumors like these reached our ears. But, having no access to correct information or contact with physicians, we believed almost all of them.

The declaration of the end of war was followed by a rumor that soldiers of the Occupation Forces would abduct women and girls. Hearing this, my neighbors packed up as many belongings as possible and fled in large numbers toward Mitsuyama.

At the end of August my husband's strength began to decline, even though he had been lucky enough to escape uninjured from the atomic bomb explosion. He had said before that he had found flea bites on his body, but I had not considered it anything serious. However, I noticed that more and more of his hair was falling out on the pillow, and when I checked the marks on his body I found that they had grown to about the size of beans. (I had read in a book somewhere that spots of this sort are an early symptom of leprosy, and so I was shocked to see that my husband had them.)

Remembering Takashi's fate, I resolved to take my husband to a doctor as quickly as possible. Fortunately my sister and her husband had come to check on us, and so we decided to leave Kawabira at once. My sister carried Naomi on her back. At first my husband walked, pulling the cart that had carried Takashi's dead body, but he soon became so exhausted that he had to get up onto the cart himself. I supported myself with a bamboo stick, my thoughts wandering here and there as I slowly made my way along the bank of the river.

The heavy rains after Takashi's death had cleaned the river and roads, reducing the pallor of the atomic bombing, but when we reached the Oide area we saw that the ruins were still smoking in some places and that only the road had been cleared. The wretched scenes of the atomic wasteland stretched away as far as the eye could see.

We walked silently through the ruins, sandwiched between the hot sun and the heat radiating from the ground. Just when we stopped to take a rest near Ohashi, the driver of a horse cart came to a halt nearby and offered to give us a ride to the Nagasaki Station area, probably out of pity at my sorry appearance. Expressing heartfelt thanks, I climbed aboard the cart.

After disembarking at the station, we walked to Sakaya-machi via Ogawa-machi only to find that not a single wooden house had survived the fires after the bombing. Across Megane-bashi

(Spectacles Bridge), however, the neighborhoods were all intact and relatives were waiting nervously at my parents' house, greeting us with cries of "you're so late!"

We lost no time in taking my husband to the relief station established at Shinkozen Primary School for medical care, but we were told that it was too late to give medical treatment because his hair was beginning to fall out and spots had appeared on his body. We went home greatly depressed. Later, we heard that Dr. Takahara was in Ginya-machi and so asked him to look at my husband. But he also said that no particular medical treatment was available.

My husband jumped fitfully to his feet many times, in a manner similar to his son, and he tried to endure the agony by splashing cold well water over his head. As his condition deteriorated, his senses seemed to become keener, and he contracted a high fever. Finally he became unable to drink water even though he was very thirsty. It was so pitiful that my sister ran several times a day for the doctor at Takahara Hospital. Seeing my husband trying desperately but unsuccessfully to drink water from a glass, I attempted time and time again to appease his thirst, even with a single drop of water, by transferring water from my mouth to his. But it did not work.

September 9

On this day, exactly one month after the death of my mother and children, we held a Buddhist service to console the souls of the dead. We invited a Buddhist priest to chant sutras. My husband, lying upstairs and apparently feeling better, said, "A priest is reading the Sukhavati Sutra" and began to chant the sutra with tears in his eyes. Then he said, "Chiyoko, Oba-chan (my mother) and the children are here to take me to the other world." Startled by these words, I asked my sister to go for Dr. Takahara. The doctor came and gave him an injection, but he had still not left the house when my husband begged feebly for water. I gave him some from my mouth, and he drank it with a gulping sound, and the next moment he took his last breath.

He wore a peaceful, slightly flushed expression, and his lips formed a smile that seemed to show that he had really ascended to heaven. I embraced his body, which was still warm, and cried bitterly, "No, my dear! Oh, no, dear! Take me with you!" To whom could I express this deep sorrow caused by the loss of my mother, my children, and now my dear husband? To whom should I open the floodgate of wrath and grief? Who should I blame? Why did we have to suffer such misery and agony? I was like a living corpse, lost in a world devoid of humanity. Even little Naomi, our only surviving child, seemed dazed and perturbed as she looked down from her aunt's back at her dead father's face.

There was no crematorium left in the ruins. Everything had been destroyed! My older sister and her husband carried my husband's corpse back to the site of our house in Shiroyama and cremated his remains on the same spot as his mother and children.

My parents' relatives eventually came back from Kazusa, a small town southeast of Nagasaki where they had moved to avoid the danger of air raids. Now our house regained some measure of liveliness, and my daughter Naomi became vivid and cheerful and soon learned to walk by herself.

If I had returned to my parents' home instead of moving to Kawabira, my son Takashi and my husband might have survived. Thoughts like this passed through my mind constantly, only intensifying my feelings of repentance and self-blame. My physical pain abated gradually, and I regained my strength little by little.

In October, my former colleagues who had been enlisted for military duty were discharged and returned home. At our school, deletions and revisions were made to the textbooks in use before the end of the war. (In January of the next year, the portrait of the Emperor and Empress that had been deified at every school was returned to the city authorities, and school textbook adjustments went into effect along with the elimination of the following subjects: ethics, geography and Japanese history.)

Around this time, demobilized soldiers, sailors and repatriates began to come home, and the railroad stations and harbor fronts bustled with activity. When I heard the loudspeakers welcoming people home I imagined that my husband and children were returning from somewhere, and I wandered in a daze around the railroad station and harbor terminal searching for a glimpse of them.

Like my husband and son, my hair thinned and purple blotches appeared on my skin.   At my brother's recommendation, I went for a medical check (as a Mitsubishi employee family member) at the Mitsubishi-run relief station for atomic bomb survivors on the site of the former Hayashi Hospital in Togiya-machi.   Tests showed my white blood cell count to be 2,800, so low that the doctors marveled that I had survived this long.   At home, my older sister prepared tea from persimmon leaves, having heard somewhere that this is an effective treatment.   She did this everyday, but even after a month my white blood cell count did not rise above 3,500.

Some time later, Mr. Arakawa (the former vice-principal at my school) made a sudden appearance and said, "Mrs. Egashira, school will soon reopen.   Will you give classes?"   I decided to accept his offer thinking that my health would only deteriorate if I continued to lie about the house mourning my dead husband and children.   Thus I began to commute to school, covering my balding head with a square of cloth and wearing a pair of baggy trousers made from my older sister's kimono.

Standing in front of the empty ruins of Shiroyama Elementary School, I was so overtaken with emotion that I could not utter a word. I could only join my hands in prayer and lower my head, letting the hot tears spill down my cheeks.

Although I remembered only the electrical cord above Mr. Arakawa's desk consumed in a thin column of fire, the flames had completely gutted the teachers' office and rushed up the stairs burning everything along the way except the principal's office and nurse's room.   Bags of rice had been piled to the ceiling in the laundry room beside the kitchen, which had been converted into an emergency storeroom, but now nothing was left.   The storeroom under the staircase and other parts of the building had also been smashed to pieces by the blast and were in a hideous state.

A total of 27 colleagues had perished in the teachers' room that now looked like a primitive cave; only three (Vice-principal Arakawa,

Sumi Miyamoto and I) had survived. In addition to the three of us, two other former teachers had survived: Mr. Yoshino, who had been off-duty that day and had escaped injury, and Mr. Sekiguchi, who had returned to Nagasaki after military duty. The five of us called together about 15 pupils who had miraculously survived.

More than 2,000 pupils had been enrolled in the school during the war, but this number had decreased to about 1,200 as a result of the compulsory evacuation of children to the countryside. The empty classrooms had been used thereafter as subsidiary Mitsubishi factories.

All of the surviving pupils had lost one or both parents. Some had lost all their relatives and were alone in the world. But each and every one seemed to be relieved to return to school and delighted to see friends again, and they stayed behind after classes to help us clean away debris. They reminded me of my dear children and in that way helped to lift my sagging spirits.

The school buildings of Nagasaki, not only those in the hypocenter but all around the city, had been destroyed by the atomic bomb explosion, and so classes were being held outdoors or on stairwells and other available spaces. Even Katsuyama Primary School and Shinkozen Primary School in central Nagasaki, which had been taken over as temporary government facilities, had moved classes to rooms in a local temple. Shiroyama Primary School resumed operation in rooms at Inasa Primary School, borrowing everything from textbooks to chalk.

The number of pupils gradually increased as families returned to the city from the countryside, first 20 then 30, and everyone joined in encouraging and comforting others.

The afflicted pupils, wearing cloth hoods to cover their heads and straw sandals with worn-out soles, made the long walk everyday between Shiroyama and Inasa. On their way home they dallied by the Urakami River to catch fish and gather river plants.

Because of the acute shortage of supplies, the children used their rationed pencils and notebooks with great care. They wore whatever rationed sneakers came their way, fully aware that they would have to go barefoot if they insisted on wearing only shoes that fit.

One day several rolls of black and white cloth were delivered to the victimized children as rationed goods. We gathered at Mr. Yoshino's home, which was located near Inasa Primary School, and spent two days cutting the cloth in order to divide it equally among the pupils. Each pupil brought his or her share home, and a few days later it reappeared as clothing, underwear and even covers for futons.

Rainy days were the most unpleasant for us because no one had an umbrella. For quite a long time after the end of the war we had to run to school dressed in our old air-raid hoods in order to keep dry. I had lost all my hoods in the atomic bombing, but one was given to each person as part of postwar relief and I was able to use this.

I longed for umbrellas when I saw pupils running through the drizzling rain with their textbooks covered in a wet cloth and held above their heads. Autumn breezes began to blow through the windows, still without glass panes, and soon winter arrived. On days when snow was falling outside, the children could only sit and listen to their teacher's words, enduring the numbness in their hands and squeezing together to keep warm.

On stormy days, when even I felt the danger of being blown into the river while crossing Inasa Bridge, I worried that my pupils might not reach school safely from Shiroyama.

It was around this time that umbrellas were rationed. But the new umbrellas were given only to people who brought a worn-out umbrella in exchange. Unlike the people living in the periphery of the hypocenter area, we had lost everything in the atomic bomb explosion and so did not have even an old handle to bring in. No matter how badly we needed one, we were unable to obtain a new umbrella.

It was the same story for rations from the army and other sources. There were some healthy survivors who, even though they had fled from the city with their belongings in a car, received clothing and blankets and then exchanged these for rice and other supplies.

"I'm giving priority to people who come to get rations with their own carts," said the official when he gave me a pair of soldier's gaiters. These were the first things given to Naomi and me by our neighborhood association after the war.

The winter vacation arrived in the midst of this chaos. I had managed to regain some measure of strength, and I remembered how my mother-in-law and husband had spoken wistfully about their hometown in the Goto Islands. After some consideration, I decided to make the trip to the village of Miiraku where my husband had been born.

I inquired here and there and finally obtained ferry tickets. With Naomi strapped to my back, and the ashes of my mother-in-law, husband and four children in a pot held tightly in my arms, I boarded the pre-dawn steamship leaving Nagasaki for the Goto Islands. My sister and her husband saw me off at the waterfront. It was my first time to board a ship of this size.

After leaving Nagasaki Harbor, the ship rocked back and forth as it made its way over the rough sea, so heavily that some passengers threw up from seasickness. I sat like a desperate refugee, clutching little Naomi in my arms, guarding the pot of ashes, and trembling with apprehension.

Unexpectedly, the steamship was unable to proceed from Fukue to Miiraku as scheduled because of the stormy conditions. I had no knowledge whatever of the geography of the Goto Islands and so almost burst into tears at having to stay in this unfamiliar place. Then an elderly man with whom I had exchanged words on the steamship asked me if I had acquaintances in some place other than Miiraku. "I recall hearing that my husband has relatives in a place called Okuura," I replied.

"It's out of my way, but you can't carry both your baby and that luggage," said the man, kindly taking some of my things and tying them skillfully onto his own luggage and then showing me the way. We walked a considerable distance along a flat road from Fukue and then climbed a steep hillside. I followed the man, holding Naomi on my back and pouring all my energy into the task of walking.

The man, who was obviously familiar with the area, greeted people along the way and asked for information about my relatives in Okuura, finally bringing me right to their door. As they say, I felt like I had "met an angel in a strange land." It was almost as though my dead husband had borrowed the form of the elderly man to guide his wife and baby to safety. I saw the man off and watched him walk away, raising my hands in prayer as he disappeared from sight.

The relatives in Okuura greeted us with tears of grief and joy, placing the pot of ashes on the large Buddhist altar in their house and caressing Naomi lovingly. To celebrate our fist visit from Nagasaki, they made special rice cakes and treated us with great hospitality.

We stayed two nights with the family In Okuura and then proceeded to Miiraku with the help of the family's son and daughter. "Uncle Minoru (my husband) used to come here on summer holidays and walk along this road wearing his college cap," said the children. I walked stoically along, listening to their stories about my husband's youth.

Small birds of some unknown species chirped in the woods as we passed, and wagtails fluttered over the sparkling water of a mountain stream. We followed the flow of the stream down a hill and then made our way over several more hills far from human settlements. We were passing through a grove of cedars when I suddenly lost consciousness. When I finally opened my eyes the children cried, "What would we have done if you died here? We were so worried!" I felt sorry for troubling them in this remote place.

But in my mind I thought about how wonderful it would be to die in this beautiful valley where my husband had apparently come every summer and winter holiday and where now I could almost feel his presence.

"That's the beach in Miiraku," said one of my companions, pointing as we crossed over the last mountain pass. But I could only look at the scene with vacant eyes.

It was a beautiful white beach scattered with clams, a site famous for its scenes of villagers pulling along oxen with water urns on their backs. There was a cemetery on the beach at Miiraku, with gravestones protruding from the sandy soil.

After burying the ashes of my family with the help of relatives, I was overcome with a desire to disappear into the depths of the ocean myself. Holding Naomi in my arms, I stood on the beach with the water lapping at my feet, not even noticing the setting sun. "Mother! Mother!" The voice of someone calling me from far beyond the red-stained clouds seemed to mingle with the sounds of the waves. Tears poured down my cheeks and I cried with all my heart.

"Mrs. Egashira! Sensei! Sensei!" Some strange force seemed to pull me back from the edge of the water. It was an illusion because there was no one else on the beach. Brought back to my senses by the sound of Naomi crying, I could only sit on the beach and weep and weep until I had no more tears to shed. And before dawn the next day, I boarded a boat from Miiraku to Fukue, listening to the "thud, thud, thud" of its engine like a beat against the bottom of the boat, and took the steamship back to Nagasaki.

During the third school term, I sometimes joined with my pupils in gazing at the scenery outdoors through the broken windows of the school. I noticed that while the children who had returned from evacuation played games cheerfully, the children exposed to the atomic bombing had a pallor of loneliness on their faces. The exposed children came to school with their heads covered with cloths. Without knowing the exact reason, they suffered from loss of hair, bleeding from the gums and dizziness.

Near the end of February, one of the laborers hired by city authorities to clear away the debris from the school reported that he had found a corpse pinned between the stairs on the third floor of the building. We all rushed to the scene and joined our hands in prayer at the sight of the unidentified corpse. How miserable it was! A badge with address, name and blood type was sewn on the work uniform, and we could decipher from this that the dead person was a girl. After that we tracked down her family and delivered the badge to her parents. "Our daughter was a student at Nagasaki Women's Commercial High School," her father explained. "Every morning she went to the temporary factory at Shiroyama Primary School as a mobilized student worker. She did not come home after the atomic bombing and so we searched for her day after day. But we did not find a trace. Sometime later we were handed some ashes that seemed to be the remains of our daughter. Now they rest on our family altar, but I have had many bad dreams since then and continued to feel uneasy about her fate. Now I finally feel relieved, and I am sure that our daughter will now be able to rest in peace." They bowed toward us over and over and expressed thanks.

Human remains were scattered about the schoolyard after the atomic bombing. The unclaimed corpses were cremated and the ashes buried on a hillock called Tsubakiyama near the teachers' room. A grave marker was erected, and services were held on the site for a long time thereafter.

On August 8, the day before the atomic bombing, I had joined several teachers in going to pick weeds in a rice paddy in the country. After the autumn harvest, members of the village young men's association delivered a bale of the rice from that paddy to the school. Later we held a memorial service for the atomic bomb dead who had participated in the weeding. The bereaved families were invited to the service, and the rice was offered on the altar. After the service the rice was divided among the bereaved families, and we all joined in remembering the victims.

Soon winter passed and the children who had studied while rubbing numb hands together to stay warm finally welcomed the arrival of spring. The time had come for the more than 30 remaining pupils to celebrate the graduation of 14 pupils, both atomic bomb survivors and returned evacuees. The graduation ceremony was held in the same way as at other schools. Three parents and five teachers were also in attendance. The national anthem was followed by addresses, but we were so consumed with sadness that we could not speak. When we sang the Japanese version of "Auld Lang Syne" and a song of gratitude, neither the teacher who provided piano accompaniment nor the singers could hold back tears. They were hot, hot tears that only the victims of the atomic bomb could shed, only the people united in this same boundless emotion.

What would become of me? What hope could I embrace? What words could I give to these children when I myself was devoid of hope and purpose? I could only hold their hands and embrace them and then bid farewell. It was the tearful parting of teachers and children who had crossed the line of death together.

At the end of the school year, after the graduation ceremony, Shiroyama Primary School was closed indefinitely. The teachers dispersed, promising to reopen the school at the Sugimoto residence in Shiroyama. The remaining pupils all officially transferred to Inasa Primary School, to which they would be commuting again in April.

Excerpt from *Nagasaki no Shogen* ("Testimonies of Nagasaki"), 1970.

My Experience of the Atomic Bombing

Raisuke Shirabe

The blast destroyed Nagasaki Medical College Hospital
(700 meters from the hypocenter), leaving only the building framework intact.

Introduction

I am deeply honored that my colleagues are planning to celebrate my *beiju* (88th birthday) on the occasion of the alumni meeting of the Nagasaki University First Department of Surgery (May 17, 1986). I considered the possibility of various gestures of gratitude but was unable to think of anything appropriate. But since the atomic bombing was the most notable event during my term of office and one which exceeds the imagination of people of the postwar period, I decided to describe my experience of the Nagasaki atomic bombing and to write an outline of its medical effects.

Innumerable descriptions of the atomic bombings have been written and so readers will already be well aware of the facts, but today, when the cry for the elimination of nuclear weapons is growing louder, I think that it will be useful to renew this awareness.

My Experience of the Atomic Bombing at Nagasaki Medical College

August 9, 1945. This is the day of the apocalypse that Nagasaki will remember forever. I had been in the hospital, on air-raid alert duty, from noon of August 8, the monthly anniversary of the Imperial Proclamation of War. Due to the absence of Dr. Takase, the team leader, I gave an order to the students on duty to be particularly watchful. I stayed overnight in the hospital.

At 6:30 a.m. on August 9, I joined Professor Naito, Professor Umeda, Professor Kido and Professor Sugiura of the pharmacy school for breakfast on the second floor of the hospital kitchen.

An air-raid alarm was sounded at seven o'clock, leaving us little time to chat. I gathered the students on duty in front of the main building, conducted a simple role call, and then sent each person to his respective post. There was no sound of enemy aircraft. The alarm was lifted at nine o'clock and changed to an air-raid alert. Still wearing gaiters, I delivered a lecture to the third-year students in the Second Middle Auditorium and then returned to my office. Passing in front of the Middle Auditorium, I saw Dr. Tsuno'o, our college president, still engaged intensively in a lecture even though it was past ten o'clock.

I returned to my office and began writing a paper. In the midst of this, I heard the drone of airplane engines. The air-raid alarm had been lifted, but it was clearly the sound of enemy airplanes. I stood up, changed from my white lab coat into a suit jacket, picked up a few things and then started for the door. Just then a pale purple light illuminated the window to the north, followed by the crash of things breaking. I hunched down like a shrimp, and the debris poured down on my back. Everything became dark. I could hear a sound resembling heavy rain, probably the sound of dirt that had been blown up into the sky by the explosion coming down in a shower. This sound stopped after a while and so I tried to get up. The debris on my back was light enough to let me stand. My eyes were open but I could not see anything in the darkness. I crouched down again and waited for the surrounding area to become silent. I cannot describe my thoughts during this morbid pause; it was like I had been left alone in the middle of hell.

I stood up again and opened my eyes. Now it was somewhat brighter, like dawn. I thought "Now!" and prepared to flee but first of all looked around. The desk where I had been writing was on its side, the filing cabinets had fallen over and the bed was out of place. Not a single piece of furniture was intact. The ceiling had collapsed and the rubble now covered everything.

I went to the front of my desk. My diary had been torn apart. I picked up the pieces and put them in my pocket. I could not find my bag, nor could I figure out what had happened to the manuscript I had been working on, my books, watch and other things. Thinking that another air raid might occur if I delayed any longer, I hurried out of the room. The hallway and stairwells were strewn with debris, but fortunately I was able to make my way downstairs.

I ran out the east entrance. A woman who had undergone surgery for appendicitis just a few days earlier was hobbling along with the support of a man, crying for help. She did not seem to have any injuries. "You are all right! Flee at once!" I shouted, running toward the air-raid shelter behind the kitchen. The boiler was crushed, and I heard the hiss of escaping steam. Two or three people were lying motionless on the concrete floor of the boiler room. Other dead people were hanging over the window frames.

On my way I ran into Professor Koyano. He had suffered two cuts on his forehead, probably caused by flying glass. Nothing serious. The cuts were two or three centimeters in length but were not bleeding badly. I greeted him with an admonition to "take care" as we passed, then hurried into the air-raid shelter. There were many people inside the shelter. Looking around, I saw Ms. Araki, a nurse in my surgery department. She had suffered a laceration of about five by three centimeters on her forearm, and this was bleeding profusely. I pulled out my handkerchief and applied a tourniquet.

I left the shelter and went to the main building, but people were flooding from the ruins and I could not get in. I turned back and began climbing the hill behind the college. I had not suffered even a scratch. I ran on, looking for acquaintances.

First, I met Katsumi Sato, a graduate student working in my department, and a nurse named Sumi. Dr. Sato was holding a cane, but he did not seem to be injured. The nurse's face was stained with blood, and she had a laceration on her hip visible through her torn trousers. They could manage to walk. I told them to flee to the hillside as quickly as possible.

Deciding to go back to my office, I cut across the college tennis court, only to meet Professor Hasegawa. He was staggering. He had a small laceration near his right eyebrow that was bleeding slightly. "Keep the wound pressed, and sit down over there," I said as I continued on my way. Next, Associate Professor Ishizaki of Koyano Surgical Department came hobbling along, with burns all over his face. He called my name in a tearful voice. He had suffered severe burns on the forearms and hands, and the skin was hanging down in shreds.

"Where were you?" I asked.

"I was in my office," he replied weakly.

"You'll be all right," I said. "Wait with Professor Hasegawa."

I hurried to the East Hospital Ward, where Dr. Kido appeared with a smile. He had apparently suffered a slight injury on the head.

A Map of Nagasaki Medical College Hospital and My Escape Route

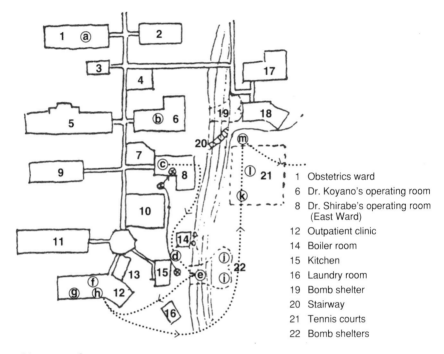

1 Obstetrics ward
6 Dr. Koyano's operating room
8 Dr. Shirabe's operating room
    (East Ward)
12 Outpatient clinic
14 Boiler room
15 Kitchen
16 Laundry room
19 Bomb shelter
20 Stairway
21 Tennis courts
22 Bomb shelters

→My route of escape
ⓧ Our emergency headquarters (twice relocated)
ⓐ Location of Dr. Naito's body
ⓑ Location of Dr. Ishizaki's body
ⓒ My location at the time of the bombing
ⓓ Where I met Dr. Kono
ⓔ The shelter where I treated Ms. Araki
ⓕ Dr. Tsuno'o's location at the time of the bombing
ⓖ Prof. Kitamura's location at the time of the bombing
ⓗ Prof. Koyano's location at the time of the bombing
ⓘ Dr. Tsuno'o's place of refuge
ⓙ Prof. Yamane's place of refuge
ⓚ Where I met Prof. Hasegawa
ⓛ Where I met Dr. Ishizaki
ⓜ Where I met Dr. Kido and Ms. Murayama

We were rejoicing over each other's survival when my head nurse, Ms. Murayama, came running up crying and calling my name. She had suffered burns on her face and arms, but they were slight in comparison to those of Dr. Ishizaki.

"Yes, good, good. Let's go up together," I said.

I heard from Dr. Kido that the nurses from my department were safe. I was relieved. Since there was no need to go to my office, I climbed the hill, helping Ms. Murayama.

The smoke engulfing the whole area indicated that fires had broken out in the hospital and nearby houses. It was like being in a thick fog. The ground that yesterday had been covered with greenery was now stripped naked. The buildings of the reformatory higher up the hill had collapsed, and fires were starting to break out in the debris. The hillside echoed with the voices of people crying for help, moaning, and calling for friends. It was a scene of terrible suffering and confusion, like an illustration depicting the agonies of hell. The wind was blowing up the hillside, covering it with a blanket of gray smoke and pushing the procession of the injured up toward the summit.

When I reached the middle of the hill near the reformatory, I heard someone calling my name to the right. It seemed that our college president, Dr. Tsuno'o, had suffered injures and had taken refuge on the hillside. Instructing Murayama and the others to go ahead, I ran toward the voice, cutting across a field and jumping down a low cliff. Dr. Tsuno'o was lying face up on the ground, his face pale and his shirt stained with fresh blood. Ms. Maeda (head nurse), Associate Professor Osajima and Dr. Takahashi were standing nearby with apprehensive expressions on their faces.

"Where are your wounds?" I asked, running up to his side.

"I suffered slight injuries on my left arm and leg," replied Dr. Tsuno'o. His voice was weak. I said, " Please hold on," and he replied, "I will be fine." The wound on his left thigh was a laceration caused by a piece of glass. It was bleeding slightly, and so I bandaged it with a piece of cloth at hand. He looked so uncomfortable wearing the bloodstained shirt that I had him take it off and gave him the shirt that I had been wearing.

The smoke was growing heavier and the fires threatened to engulf us at any minute. Fires had already broken out in the Sakamoto-machi area below, and the cracks and pops of the burning debris seemed to be coming from right beside us. We could not remain where we were. I had Dr. Takahashi lift Dr. Tsuno'o onto his back, and I led the way up toward the top of the hill. Dr. Tsuno'o was more pallid than ever, and he suffered nausea and vomited several times as we ascended the hill. Dr. Tsuno'o himself spoke up, attributing the nausea to brain anemia. We had to rest several times and so our progress was slow.

We finally arrived at a safe spot halfway up Mt. Kompira. There had been a sweet potato patch here before, but now the leaves and stems of the potato plants were torn to shreds and the bare ground was exposed. We had Dr. Tsuno'o lie down in the middle of the patch. Fortunately, we were able to cover him with a quilt that someone had brought. There was a stiff breeze, and he looked cold. Dr. Okura soon came along, looking healthy, and built a hut from the potato vines and put up a "headquarters" flag nearby.

About this time the wind changed direction. The smoke cleared, allowing a clear view of the area below. The nurses' dormitory, the hospital corridors, the basic science building and other structures were engulfed in flames. The sun was stained a sickening brownish-red color. People's faces were also blackish red, as though tinted with sunset colors.

Somebody brought a first-aid bag. I found ampules of iodine inside and used these to treat the president's wounds. He had two lacerations on the head and four on the left thigh, plus countless others small cuts all over his body. I spread iodine over the wounds. The three-by-five centimeter laceration on his left buttocks was sullied with dirt and so I rinsed it with libanol solution. He began to feel better, and the nausea subsided. The wounds on his hand were also due to glass splinters. Two were cuts of about 1.5 cm x 0.5 cm on the back of the hand, and the other was a cut on the knuckle of the middle finger. These had already been disinfected by Dr. Ichinose, and so I left them the way they were.

The wind began once again to blow up toward the top of the

My Movements Around the Medical College and Surrounding Hillside

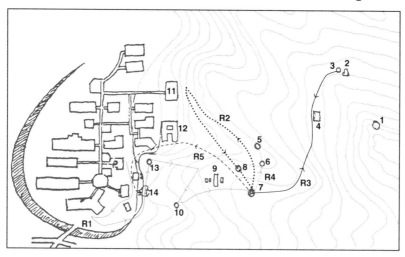

1.	The Anakobo area	
2.	A nearby house	
3.	Where the students cooked rice	
4.	Anakobo Temple	
5.	Where Dr. Nagai and I slept	
6.	Location of our discussions on the night of August 9	
7.	Where Dr. Tsuno'o slept	
8.	Where I treated Dr. Nagai
9.	The reformatory
10.	Where I first saw Dr. Tsuno'o
11.	Psychiatric ward
12.	Nurses' dormitory
13.	Where I met Dr. Hasegawa and others
14.	The bomb shelter behind the kitchen

Route 1   My route of escape immediately after the bombing

Route 2   The path I took as I searched for my son and then went off to treat Dr. Nagai

Route 3   The route I took to pick up supplies of dry bread and rice

Route 4   The path I took to the night shelter after the meeting on the night of August 9

Route 5   Dr. Tsuno'o's route down to the bomb shelter on August 10 mountain. Rain began to fall, like a passing shower, but not heavily enough to warrant action. The wounded on the hillside were all shivering from the rain and wind. I took a break and went to look for my son Koji (a first-year medical student) on the other hill across a small valley. In the recess of the mountain, I found Dr. Ishizaki lying like a corpse bundled up in a white hospital quilt. I could not carry him alone. A patient from my clinic had escaped injury and fled to the valley with his wife to avoid the rain. When I greeted him, he responded happily and gave me a handful of cigarettes.

I went to the hill behind the psychiatric department, crying "Koji!" in a loud voice, but there was no answer. I shuddered, thinking that he had perhaps been trapped under the debris of the auditorium and perished in the subsequent fire.

There were innumerable people, injured beyond any hope of help, lying in the fields and on the roadside. Most of them could not even talk. A fourth-year medical student named Oku was lying at the bottom of a cliff. He seemed to be unconscious and would not answer my calls. Rainwater was dripping from overhanging weeds onto his face but he did not wipe it away. He did not have long to live. A third-year student named Ueno was wearing a bandage on his head. Although not as energetic as usual, he was attending diligently to the needs of a friend. Dr. Hidaka of my department was uninjured and kindly assisted in my search for Koji. But, as I feared, it was to no avail.

After a while I heard a voice calling my name from the hillside where the president was lying. "Dr. Nagai's bleeding won't stop, please come," cried the voice. Running back to the hillside, I found that Dr. Nagai (Takashi) had suffered a fingertip-sized laceration on the right side of his face beside the ear and that this was bleeding profusely. Two postgraduate students from the radiology department had been trying unsuccessfully to stop the flow of blood. Several pairs of forceps were dangling from the wound. I sensed a lofty dignity in the attitude of Dr. Nagai, who did not as much as frown during the operation without anesthesia. I took over and tried to apply the forceps, but my attempts were also futile. I had no alternative but to press a tampon firmly into the wound and to suture the skin over it.   This finally brought the bleeding to a stop.

When the procedure was over, Dr. Nagai took the radiology assistants and nurses down the hill and directed the construction of a hut for shelter at night near the foot of a stone embankment wall.   Dr. Nagai was a Christian, and he indeed looked like Jesus leading his disciples on a pilgrimage.

I went back to check on the president and found him lying still and silent.   Somebody brought a piece of ice in a container made from a pumpkin shell cut in half, and we urged Dr. Tsuno'o to eat it. He must have been thirsty because he ate the ice with relish.

I think it was about four o'clock in the afternoon when a third-year student named Koda arrived from the foot of the hillside carrying Professor Takagi on his back.   Dr. Takagi had no wounds, but his face was ashen and he had no strength whatever.   It seemed that he had been in his office at the time of the explosion.   The building collapsed, trapping him underneath, but he had fortunately been able to break through the ceiling and escape.   He had crossed the sports field and made his way toward Urakami Cathedral only to run out of strength at the riverside.   Koda had found him lying there. We made a bed for him beside the president.   I conducted an examination but found no wounds or broken bones.   Moreover, there was nothing unusual in his chest or abdominal sounds.   Still he complained vehemently about his discomfort.   His pulse was fast and faint.   I assumed that he was in a state of shock.

Professor Kiyoki of the pharmacology department came along soon after, climbing toward the headquarters flag with the aid of a cane.   He reported that he had been digging an air-raid shelter at the time of the explosion.   He had luckily escaped death because he had been taking a rest inside the shelter, but he had been struck in the lower back by a piece of falling lumber.   He had been wearing only a pair of shorts at the time and so was very lucky not to have suffered any burns.   It was another case of "fortune in the midst of misfortune."

In the evening, Dr. Egami (associate professor in the ear, nose and throat department) and Kawamoto (an assistant in the hospital pharmacy) came along healthy and fully dressed.   Both had been at home in the suburb of Nameshi and so had escaped injury, but, overcome with worry about the situation at the medical college, they had arrived here after a long trek through the wasteland. They brought some medical supplies and treated two or three people, but after a while I did not see them anymore.

The rain subsided, and an evening mist began to cover the area. The wind also seemed to let up. Fires were burning more fiercely than ever in the neighborhoods below. As night fell the red glow increased, and the sea of fire stretched as far as the eye could see. The number of people ascending Mt. Kompira dwindled, most of the refugees having found spots to rest on the hillsides. Dr. Tsuno'o and Professor Takaki were ready to spend the night just where they were lying. A number of college staff and other injured people were lying nearby. Associate Professor Nagai and his group were in their hut at the embankment wall; Ms. Michijima, head nurse in the dermatology department, and her group were lying on the field below Anakobodera (Buddhist temple); a group of nurses had found a place within the temple precincts; and another group of students and nurses had accumulated in the garden of a demolished house nearby. Everyone nestled close to his or her neighbor, encouraging each other and preparing to pass a dark lonely night. Many of the people who had climbed the hillside probably continued up to heaven. At the site of the reformatory, an injured goat was crying pathetically, and in the evening two white goats arrived from somewhere and scrounged for food.

That night the wind died down completely, and the sky was so clear that the stars stood out in relief. There was no moon, and nothing was visible in the pitch darkness. I had not eaten anything since breakfast, and although I had not even noticed it in the midst of all the horror and stress, I was so hungry that my stomach was rumbling. I felt unbearable pity for all the other people on the hillside who must also have been famished.

Just around that time, people from relief headquarters in the center of Nagasaki brought a box of dry bread. I immediately carried this around to each camp, searching for the paths from memory and passing out a packet of bread to each person I met in the darkness. I became choked with emotion at the sight of people lying despondently in the cold night, and I could not find any words of solace to offer them. Answering questions as best as I could about lost friends, I made my way through the darkness until arriving at my last stop, the house below Anakobodera.

Led by a fourth-year student named Anto, the group here was cooking white rice in a large pot that they had retrieved from the ruins of the house with the owner's permission. The four or five young women in wartime trousers assisting in this activity, I heard, were mobilized student-workers at the Mitsubishi factories. It moved me to see their efforts. If only because of the campfire, this spot alone was bright and warm.

While speaking with the students about the events of the day, I realized that Professor Sofune was lying alone in a nearby field. I searched for him, calling his name, and brought him back to the group of students at the house. His injuries were light, but like Professor Takaki he was suffering terribly. I made a bed for him beside the fire and asked the students to attend to him.

When the rice was ready we made rice balls and placed these in the box used to distribute dried bread. Then Anto and I distributed these as we made our way back to where Dr. Tsuno'o was resting. The hillside was darker than ever, and it took us at least 30 minutes to walk about the distance of about one kilometer. It was probably past ten o'clock. The people resting here were quiet but still awake. The president ate the rice balls I gave him with gusto, and I felt reassured about his recovery.

The fires in the neighborhoods below had died down to a certain extent, but bright red flames were still visible darting from broken windows. It was a captivating sight, one that reminded me of how the city of Nagasaki had been so beautiful and full of life before this fateful day.

To relieve my hunger, I had dug up sweet potatoes. I chewed on these while running back and forth across the hillside, and then I ate four or five rice balls that filled my stomach. The achievements of the Mitsubishi student workers and Anto deserve the highest praise. I can only offer my utmost thanks.

After the food had been distributed, I assembled the uninjured associate professors and discussed the plan for tomorrow, keeping warm by the campfire.   The plan was as follows:

1) Prepare two stretchers early in the morning and carry the president and Professor Takagi to my house.
2) Make a list of the college staff who are camping.
3) Have Anto prepare breakfast.
4) Organize a communication group and make contact with the city relief headquarters.
5) Report to Professor Koyano.

The night grew late.   We decided to sleep.   I accepted Dr. Nagai's invitation and found a place to sleep on the straw in the makeshift hut made by the radiology department staff.

Looking up at the ceiling, I quietly recalled the day's events. It was like a dream.   In a flash of light the world had been thrown into a state of chaos and countless numbers of people had fallen injured or died instantly.   We managed to escape to this safe spot on the hillside, but the hospital and neighborhoods around it had all burned to ashes and now we had no place of work.   What on earth were we to do from tomorrow?

"Today I met Dr. Tsuno'o, Professor Koyano, Professor Takagi, Professor Hasegawa, and Professor Sofune, but what has become of the other professors?   My second son Koji was undoubtedly in a lecture at the basic science building.   Did he escape?   If he managed to escape he would have fled, not to this Anakobodera area, but to the hillside behind Urakami Cathedral via the college sports field.   If, from there, he fled in the direction of the seminary and proceeded to Michino'o past the rear of the teachers' college, he is probably safe. But I wonder if he was aware of the route?   And how about my eldest son Seiichi, who is working at the Ohashi Arms Factory?   I hope he is safe. . ."   Absorbed with thoughts like this, my mind revolved like a kaleidoscope and I could not fall asleep.

After a while, an enemy airplane flew overhead and bombed the Michino'o area.   It was a minor raid.   The airplane also dropped some strange kind of bomb that exploded in the sky above us.   There were no further air raids, and I fell asleep not knowing the time.   I had lost my watch and so cannot say exactly, but it was probably around twelve o'clock at night.

(The above is the exact content of my diary written soon after the atomic bombing. From August 10 I began to write in greater detail, and so I will present only the main points here.)

August 10

The sky is clear today, unmarred by even a wisp of cloud. Dr. Nagai and his group got up early in the morning and marched to the pharmacology department's air-raid shelter in orderly formation. I visited the college president and found him in unexpectedly good spirits. Professor Takaki, however, was still very sick.

Knowing that the college president's official residence and family in Nishiyama were safe, I suggested that we carry him home by stretcher, but the president would not agree, rather insisting that he could not receive proper treatment at home. With no choice but to follow his wishes, I decided to take him down to the hospital for the time being at least. But the buildings were completely gutted, and there was barely a place to step amid the debris. For lack of any other refuge, we carried both Dr. Tsuno'o and Professor Takaki to the cave shelter and placed them there, still lying on their stretchers.

Professor Koyano came along at this point, and Dr. Tsuno'o asked him to take over as acting college president.

I left to check on the state of the college. Going first to my own office, I found that the interior had burned and crumbled and that nothing at all was left. The books on the shelf were still smoldering. The losses were as follows: the futon (bedding) I had brought in to use while on duty, my Londin watch, a leather brief-case containing bank passbooks, records of published papers, and various resource materials. They were all things that I could not do without.

The hospital wards were all in a similar state, and the outdoor corridors were strewn with corpses. A few survivors were wandering about like sleepwalkers, while others were crawling along the ground seeking help.

The basic science buildings, most of which had been made entirely of wood, had burned to ashes. Only one corpse, probably that of the administrative official Mr. Yamaki, was lying in the ruins. I continued to the burned out site of the forensic medicine department. There was also a corpse here, probably that of Professor Kunifusa. I raised my hands in prayer at the sight.

On the college sports field, where the staff of the radiology department had been raising vegetables, I found the corpses of several nurses lying on the ground in their soiled uniforms. It was a heartrending sight.

Passing beside the psychiatry department on my way back from the sports field, I heard from a student that Professor Yamane was lying in the depths of the air-raid shelter. Removing him from the shelter, I found that someone had wrapped filthy bandages around his head and face and that he had lost all strength. I administered first-aid and gave him an injection of a heart stimulating drug, then reported his condition to Professor Koyano.

There were many other injured people, but it was impossible to provide adequate treatment in the ruins. I conferred with Professor Koyano about setting up a relief station in Nameshi, where my family had evacuated prior to the bombing. Receiving his consent, I left the college at about one o'clock and walked to Nameshi where I visited Mr. Kataoka, chairman of the community association, to ask for his cooperation. We discussed various possibilities, but it seemed that the local Shinto shrine was the only realistic alternative. I also met with the chairman of the community association in the adjacent neighborhood of Ito-cho and received his permission to use a building called the "Iwaya Club."

With these arrangements in place, I returned to the Shishaku family residence where my family was living temporarily. They saw me approach and came out to greet me: my son Seiichi (18) bandaged from head to foot, wife Sumiko (40), second daughter Choko (14), third daughter Reiko (12) and fourth daughter Junko (8). My second son Koji (16) was nowhere in sight. He had not returned from the

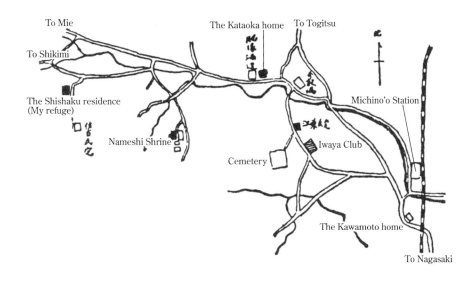

To Mie

To Shikimi

The Kataoka home   To Togitsu

The Shishaku residence
(My refuge)

Michino'o Station

Nameshi Shrine

Iwaya Club

Cemetery

The Kawamoto home

To Nagasaki

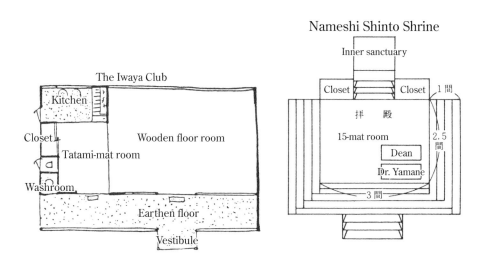

The Iwaya Club

Kitchen

Closet

Tatami-mat room

Wooden floor room

Washroom

Earthen floor

Vestibule

Nameshi Shinto Shrine

Inner sanctuary

Closet   Closet   1 間

拝　　殿

15-mat room   2.5
間

Dean

Dr. Yamane

3 間

college.

The house was located about four kilometers from the atomic bomb hypocenter, but the ceiling had collapsed and all the windows had been smashed at the time of the explosion. I was relieved to see that my eighty-year-old mother was fine. Having apparently spent the night sick with worry, my family greeted me with tears of joy. That night, caught in an endless conversation about the events of the past two days, I forgot the passage of time and got little sleep.

The Burns Suffered by My Son Seiji

Seiji had suffered burns to his entire back, but his upper arms were fine, possibly due to the fact that his shirt sleeves had been rolled up at the time. An explanation for the burns to his lower right arm may be that he had been drawing a picture with that hand and his body had been slightly tilted in that direction. The burns were second degree, and I could not see any glass fragments or signs of infection.

August 11

I arranged for repairs to the Iwaya Club and left for the college to collect the wounded. After establishing a reception in front of the outpatient clinic, I had the surviving staff draw up a list of the wounded, dead and missing and had them convey this information to the people who came looking for relatives.

After paying a visit to the college president and Professor Takaki, I launched an investigation into the whereabouts of the missing faculty members. I was delighted to find that Professor

Kunifusa, whom I had assumed to be dead, had in fact survived. He was lying on the floor in the dermatology department, his wife cooling his head with water drawn from a well into a can. He was burning with fever. I drew water into a large bucket and gave this to his wife, urging her to do whatever she could because he would not be able to endure this condition for long.

I was speaking later with Professor Koyano when a fourth-year student named Matsuse informed us that he had found a corpse that seemed to be Dr. Naito. He showed me the handbook that he had found in the pocket, and sure enough it seemed to be that of Professor Katsutoshi Naito. I went to the gynecology department and found the professor's corpse lying beside a fallen beam in the corridor. He was lying curled up like a shrimp. There was a blackish-red mark on wall nearby, apparently a handprint made from blood. Dr. Naito had probably been hit on the head with the beam and then made the print with his own blood.

A decision had still not been reached about whom to place in the relief station. The president was still insisting on staying here instead of going home. On the basis of an examination, Professor Sano concluded that Professor Takaki was in such a serious condition that he would probably not survive a long trip by stretcher. Finally we decided to carry Professor Kunifusa home by stretcher, to place Dr. Tsuno'o and Dr. Yamane in the relief station, and to assign the task of selecting student helpers to Dr. Kido.

That evening, I enlisted eight surviving nurses (Abe, Kida, Deguchi, Sakai, Sasayama, Honda, Murakami and Yaguchi) to help me carry medical supplies from beneath the burned out floor of the Shirabe Surgical Department and to load these onto the cart that Mr. Sako of Nameshi had kindly provided. After that I walked back to the Shishaku residence in Nameshi. Due to the sudden increase in people, the eight nurses were forced to lie side-by-side in the six-mat room. For food, I asked Mr. Kawamoto, an employee in the college hospital pharmacy, to go to the relief headquarters set up at Ibi-no-kuchi to obtain rice rations. The nurses, exhausted from their efforts of the past day, fell into a deep sleep soon after dinner.

August 12

The nurses left early in the morning to clean the Iwaya Club building and the Shinto shrine. In the afternoon we carried the medical supplies and made preparations to receive the wounded. However, some trouble was encountered in arranging for the truck and they did not arrive until the middle of the night. Like the nurses, I was sound asleep at the Shishaku residence and so did not hear about their arrival until the morning of August 13.

August 13

I received the news about the arrival of the wounded. The president and Professor Yamane had been placed, still on their stretchers, in a six-mat room, with the accompanying students lying nearby. I ordered some of the students to rush to my home and bring two sets of bedding back to the shrine, and then made both the president and Professor Yamane comfortable in the interior. Ms. Maeda, head nurse of Tsuno'o Medical Department, was looking after Dr. Tsuno'o but needed help, and so I asked one of the nurses from my department to join her.

The physician in charge of treatment was Professor Kido, who enlisted the help of several third-year students (Ueno, Ebisaki, Katayama, Kobayashi, Narubayashi and Yamamoto). They worked assiduously alongside the nurses, not only treating burns and wounds but also assisting patients with meals and bodily wastes. It was like a battlefield clinic.

Since no sterilization equipment was available, they sterilized instruments by placing them in water boiled in wash basins on charcoal stoves, and dipped gauzes in hot water containing antiseptic. There were no pots or pans either, and so they had to cook food in buckets. Professor Yamane did not show signs of fever but from the afternoon developed mild stiffness of the jaw, raising concerns that he was suffering from tetanus. At home, my son Seiichi was moaning with pain, and my daughter Junko was in the kitchen preparing meals for about 15 people all by herself.

August 14

The patients at Iwaya Club were all in a serious condition, suffering from high fever and diarrhea and even from bloody stools. We jumped to the conclusion that it was dysentery, and isolated these patients in a corner of the room. However, they began to die one after another, and the students were thrown into a frenzy gathering pieces of wood and cremating the remains. As if that was not enough, we received requests for house calls from families in the neighborhood, and a student would have to take a nurse and go to each house to treat wounds or to give injections of heart-stimulating drugs.

The president continued to suffer from a high fever and the added discomfort of diarrhea. Professor Yamane's jaw stiffness was worse than ever. I gave him an injection of serum received from Dr. Tsuno'o but it had no effect whatsoever. Every time someone came to the shrine for worship and rang the bell, he suffered a sudden spasm of the back muscles. He could swallow neither food nor medicine. It was painful to watch him suffer. The worst thing was that, although fond of sake, he was unable even to take a sip.

Seiichi's condition remained unchanged, his moaning not letting up even for a second. We heard nothing about Koji. We were so busy attending to the wounded in the daytime that we hardly had time even to remember, but when we sat down to an dinner in the eerie light of rapeseed oil lamps, we spoke in sad, lifeless voices.

August 15

Professor Yamane's tetanus became critical. By afternoon he began to lose consciousness, and shortly after 7:00 p.m. he finally joined the ranks of the dead. It is hard to imagine how Dr. Tsuno'o, who was lying beside him, felt when he witnessed the death of his colleague.

I was walking on the road in the afternoon when I heard from local residents that the war had ended. We had no radio and so had been unaware of the Emperor's announcement of surrender at noon. I conveyed the news to the nurses at dinner, and they fell into a morbid silence, moving their chopsticks mechanically.

August 16

Seiichi's condition deteriorated to the brink of death. His cries to his mother became weaker and weaker until he took his last breath around noon, as though falling asleep. Several people from the neighborhood helped me carry him to a nearby hillside and to cremate his remains. I had often heard him talking with his younger brother, repeating the wartime maxim that "Ours are lives of 20 years," but as it turned out his was a life of only 18 years.

After the cremation, I immediately went to visit the president and students and also responded to house calls with a nurse whenever requested. It was an emergency situation, and I could not hide at home and wallow in personal grief.

Dr. Tsuno'o began to suffer terribly from diarrhea, causing great concern for Ms. Maeda (the head nurse) attending to him. I called for Dr. Osajima and asked him to provide internal treatment.

August 17

Dr. Shigeru Tsuno'o, the brother of our college president and a professor of pharmacology at Showa Medical School, arrived from Tokyo to take care of his brother. He immediately took the president's temperature. When I asked him the result, he said "39 degrees" but showed me the thermometer, which registered a temperature of 41 degrees. He obviously assumed that the truth would only cause his brother unnecessary anxiety. "If I could only sweat, my fever would come down," lamented the president.

A rumor went around today that the American forces were about to land on Japanese shores, and many of the residents of the

Nameshi neighborhood including the Shishaku family gathered up mosquito nets and foodstuffs and fled to the forests of Mt. Iwaya. Around seven o'clock, after dinner, I received a request to make a house call to one of our neighbors. I found an elderly man with a cut of about 10 cm in length on his left cheek, lying on the bloodstained tatami mats. I took a piece of cloth at hand and pressed it against the wound, then told one of the family members to run to the relief station (a distance of about two kilometers) to fetch my suturing equipment. In the meantime, Mr. Kataoka of the neighborhood appeared and said, "Dr. Shirabe, I suggest that you ignore that patient and flee as quickly as possible. The police were among the first to run away. As a physician I could not do anything so irresponsible, and so I waited for the equipment and finished the task of suturing the wound.

When I returned home I found my daughters trembling with fear (about an impending American invasion). I told them not to worry. I also went to the relief station and urged the nurses to fulfill their duties.

August 18

At the relief station, the nurses begged me to let them go home. They were terribly afraid about the threat of an American invasion, perhaps because they were dimly aware of the atrocities committed by Japanese troops on the Chinese continent. Thinking that I would have no excuse to give their parents if anything happened to them, even though they had managed to survive the atomic bombing, I conferred with Dr. Kido and with him decided to close the relief station.

As a result the surviving patients were transferred to hospitals in Isahaya and Omura, and the nurses were able to depart for their family homes. Although lasting for only six days, our relief activities had been tantamount to medical work on the battlefield, and we were all mentally and physically exhausted from the hectic schedule. I decided to hold a party at the Shishaku residence, partly to mark the end of the relief station, partly to express thanks for the selfless efforts of the staff.

Since the nurses had all departed, the participants consisted of about five or six people including Dr. Kido and the medical students Ueno and Katayama. We cooked the two chickens that had been raised by my sons and obtained, somewhat forcibly, a bottle of saké from the Hizuka Winery. Our little party, held in the silence of a neighborhood where not a single resident now remained, probably also served as a kind of wake for my two dead sons.

August 22

(The death of Dr. Tsuno'o, president of Nagasaki Medical College)
After the closure of the relief station, my duties became very light, confined to care for Dr. Tsuno'o who was still lying in the Shinto shrine and to a few house calls.

The president's cuts from glass splinters had healed for the most part, leaving internal symptoms such as diarrhea and fever as his principle ailments. Dr. Tsuno'o seems to have taken control of his own treatment at this point, with the help of Associate Professor Osajima. But the high fever and a lack of appetite persisted, and from the 19th he developed an inflammation of the oral mucosa and purple epidermal blotches. His general malaise worsened, and by the afternoon of the 21st he began to lose consciousness. Finally, at around ten o'clock on the morning of August 22, he passed away. At his beside were his wife, his brother, Professor Koyano, Associate Professor Osajima and several other department staff members, Associate Professor Kido and my wife and me. We could only shed helpless tears, sitting beside the bed shocked and bewildered. In my diary that day, I wrote, "A great star has fallen to Earth. This is my true feeling: The death of Dr. Tsuno'o, who was both an accomplished scholar and skillful administrator, is a great loss not only for Nagasaki Medical College but for the entire education system of Japan."

We carried the remains back to the college and held a simple wake in the lobby of the ruined outpatient clinic, then conducted a funeral the following day and cremated the remains on the tennis court behind the college.

August 28

This was the day that we miraculously discovered the remains of my second son, Koji. Exhausted from the relief activities of several straight days, I lost my energy and found it more and more difficult to respond to the requests for house calls. But I could not sit still when I remembered my duty as a physician in an emergency, and so I continued the treatment of the dying atomic bomb injured, dragging my heavy feet along the paths to their homes.

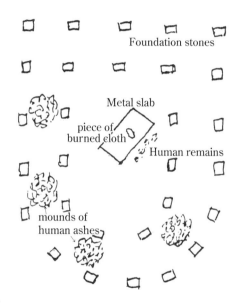

Foundation stones

Metal slab

piece of burned cloth

Human remains

mounds of human ashes

On August 28, when things had settled, I took my wife Sumiko and daughters to the ruins of the medical college to search for traces of our son Koji. Having heard that the first-year students had been in the middle of an anatomy lecture at the time of the bombing, we searched for the auditorium but could find nothing, the wooden buildings having burned to the ground and now only the foundations remaining. Several hundred crows were flying in the sky overhead, scouring the ground below for the flesh of the dead, their voices like angry curses emitted by the spirits of the departed. It was a macabre scene.

The auditorium had been reduced to ashes, leaving only two rows of foundation stones. Three or four piles of human ashes were visible amid the stones. We were picking up shreds of ashes from each pile,

The Piece of My Son's Clothing that We Found

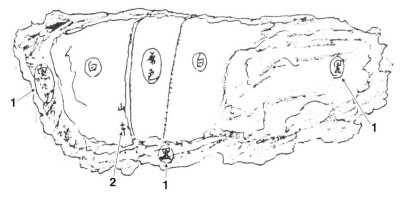

1 This part had been scorched black.
2 The name of my nephew was written here.
This confirmed for us that it was a piece of Koji's clothing.

having no idea to whom they belonged, when my youngest daughter Junko called out in a loud voice, "There is something here!" Running to the spot, I found a piece of burned cloth stuck to a fallen rectangular metal panel, apparently the door to the auditorium. Closer inspection revealed this to be the part of a pair of blue serge trousers containing the belt hook. Sewn to this was a patch of white cloth with the letters "Yamamoto" written in black ink. "These are Koji's trousers!" exclaimed my wife Sumiko. Yamamoto was the only son of my eldest sister, Tamano. He had been drafted to serve as a naval medical officer after graduating from Kyushu University Medical School and was stationed in Rabaul, a naval base in the South Pacific. Koji had received his school uniforms as a gift. All of the other students had been wearing khaki workman's uniforms. Koji was the only one wearing a blue serge student uniform, and so we knew for certain that we had found our son's remains. It seemed that he had fallen face down on the door and that his body had burned to ashes, only a patch of cloth from his trousers escaping the flames.

September 3

After confirming the death of Koji, I became totally drained of energy and could hardly bring myself to do anything. Comforted and encouraged by my wife and children, I spent several days making my usual house calls, but I trudged along lethargically like a sleepwalker.

On September 2 a request came for a house call in Yokomichi, a distance of about two kilometers. I wanted to refuse, feeling so sluggish that I could barely walk, but I went out of pity for the atomic bomb survivor. My progress was so slow that it took me more than an hour to reach my destination. The patient was on the brink of death, but I administered an injection. I heard later that the man had died soon after I left for home.

On September 3 I received a message from the college headquarters asking me to report there at once for an important meeting regarding the re-establishment of the college. I wanted to go but was not confident about making the trip by myself, and so I asked my daughter Choko to accompany me. We left the house and walked about two kilometers to Michino'o Station, where we caught a train into Nagasaki. From Nagasaki Station we walked another kilometer to the Chamber of Commerce and Industry, where the college headquarters had been temporarily established. In Ogawa-machi, on the way, I saw Associate Professor Osajima walking about ten meters ahead of us. Assuming that he was also on his way to the meeting, I tried to catch up with him but could not. Nor could I muster up a voice loud enough to call him. As a result we maintained the same distance all the way the Chamber of Commerce and Industry, arriving there with a sigh of relief. I got the impression that Dr. Osajima was suffering from the same kind of weakness as me.

The meeting lasted for a little more than two hours, and I left for home with Choko at my side. But by the time I reached home I was feeling so ill that I collapsed in bed.

The following morning I discovered a countless number of small purple blotches on my upper arms and thighs. These were the same color as those I had seen on all the atomic bomb victims who had subsequently died. Now it was my turn; I shuddered with apprehension.

Professor Kitamura called at our door for some reason, and so I showed him my spots. He said, "I have them too" and rolled up his sleeve to show me. His were somewhat darker in color than mine, but unlike me he was in good spirits. Then my wife Sumiko came along and said, "They are probably flea bites, because I have some too." She showed me her spots with a compassionate expression on her face, but they were different from mine. Just in case, I had my daughter Choko, just turned 14 years of age, give me an intravenous injection of vitamin C. I also had her give me an injection of 20 cc calcium for my sore throat. She administered the injections skillfully, but the sites of the injections turned into spots that would not fade away. This was another source of worry.

For a week after that I looked at the spots on my arms and thighs, wondering what would become of my family after my death and thinking about drawing up a last will and testament. It was agonizing. I had no appetite. My body was so sluggish that I could not even turn over in bed. I tended to remain silent because I had trouble working up the energy to speak.

After about a week, however, the spots on the injection sites began to change color, turning from purple to blue and then to yellow, and I began to think, "I may survive after all." This was around September 12 or 13. It was an exhilarating feeling.

I think it was around September 16 that Hiroshi Fujii, a staff member in my department, came for a visit and checked my blood count. My red and white blood cell count was 3.5 million and 2,400 respectively, probably much higher than at the time when my spots were at their peak. It filled me with dread when I learned later that almost all of the people whose white blood cell count fell below 1,000 had perished. Fujii also brought along a beer bottle filled with beef broth that I drank with great relish.

Around September 20, a third-year student named Koda came along and asked to be put up for the night. I happily agreed, if only because we were feeling lonely after the death of our two sons, but I regretted this decision somewhat because he was a chatterbox and would not leave me alone. Feeling weak and unable to engage in conversation, I was lying there hoping that he would soon fall asleep when he found a bottle of alcohol in the vestibule and asked me if he could drink it. "If you die as result, don't hold me responsible," I replied. "There's no need to worry because this is ethyl, not methyl alcohol," he said, pouring out a small amount into a wine glass and diluting it with glucose. He urged me to join him. I declined at first, thinking it unwise in view of the damage to my liver, but he was so persistent that I took a few sips. This tasted wonderful in my mouth, and I drank a whole glassful. My body warmed up, and I found that I could talk without getting tired.

Considering this concoction to be medicine, I drank a small amount at breakfast and dinner every day after that and, perhaps as a result, gradually regained my strength. My wife Sumiko also commented that I looked much better. Well, if I could heal my illness with wine, which I did not dislike, there could be nothing better. Now the bottle of alcohol that had been left to sit in our vestibule seemed like a precious commodity. For me, it was a saving grace. Only after imbibing this liquid did I begin to regain my strength and to feel confident about my recovery.

After escaping from death, I lounged around the Shishaku residence ruminating. I had somehow managed to survive, but my sons Seiichi and Koji would never return to enjoy their youth. What was to become of the Shirabe family? More importantly, what sort of fate awaited Nagasaki Medical College, which now lay in ruins? Would it be re-established? And would I return to my former post? There was barely a single ray of sunshine in the midst of all this gloomy speculation. September 24 arrived, but I still had neither the energy nor the courage to visit the college.

A photo of the mushroom cloud taken from one of the American planes.

The hypocenter area as it looked two days before the atomic bombing.

U.S. Armed Forces photograph
From the collection of the Nagasaki Atomic Bomb Museum

The same area three days after the bombing.

U.S. Armed Forces photograph
From the collection of the Nagasaki Atomic Bomb Museum

The road to Urakami Cathedral winds through the scorched landscape.

Photograph by Shigeo Hayashi
From the collection of the Nagasaki Atomic Bomb Museum

The view from a hill near the atomic bomb hypocenter.

Photograph by Shigeo Hayashi
From the collection of the Nagasaki Atomic Bomb Museum

The "torii" gate at Sanno Shrine (800 meters from the hypocenter)
lost one of its legs but remained standing.

Photograph by Shigeo Hayashi
From the collection of the Nagasaki Atomic Bomb Museum

Children whose hair fell out due to radiation exposure.

U.S. Armed Forces photograph
From the collection of the Nagasaki Atomic Bomb Museum

A treatment room inside the emergency relief facility set up in Shinkohzen Primary School.

Photograph by Torahiko Ogawa
From the collection of the Nagasaki Atomic Bomb Museum

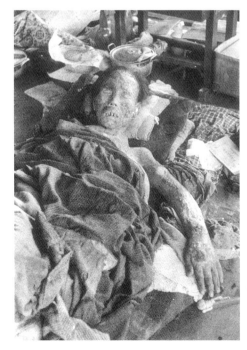

*A woman with horrible
burns lies on the floor
at the Shinkohzen relief facility.*

Photograph by Eiichi Matsumoto
Courtesy of the Asahi Newspaper Company

A woman carries the cremated remains of a relative to a memorial service.

Photograph by Eiichi Matsumoto
Courtesy of the Asahi Newspaper Company

A mother and her children cremating one of their relatives.

Photograph by Eiichi Matsumoto
Courtesy of the Asahi Newspaper Company

The Human Dam

Chie Setoguchi

The Urakami River flowing under Motoh Bridge

I was very distraught as I left the house and started down the hillside. This was the house where I had sought refuge with my children after evacuating the city during the war. I had come today to fetch our winter clothes, only to be told by the owner of the house that they had been stolen in the confusion after the atomic bombing. I had no choice but to turn away empty-handed.

"Maybe I should go back and ask him if that big parcel I saw in the corner is our clothing," I thought to myself as I made my way along the narrow path behind Fuchi Shinto Shrine. "I should have come and asked for our things right after the bombing. I suppose that it was my own fault. If I had taken time from work and come I wouldn't have had to listen to that man say, 'If you leave something unattended for more than ten days, it should be no surprise when it disappears.'" But my pangs of remorse were overshadowed by the knowledge that I was very lucky to still be alive. I realized the futility of dwelling on this simple loss and made up my mind to forget about the whole affair as quickly as possible.

I noticed the ruins of the steel works below me in the valley, and I examined the demolished steel forge inside the twisted frame of the building as if looking at naked entrails through a deformed ribcage. The factory had sent flames to the sky for three days after the bombing. But the embers were cold now, just as the screams of anguish echoing in the factory had now fallen silent. Only the relentless summer sun was unaffected, beating down on the grass, trees and rocks stained a strange muddy-brown hue.

The city of Nagasaki was a monotony of rubble as far as the eye could see. The surrounding mountains managed to maintain some dignity, although only beyond a certain distance. Buildings had been completely leveled except for a few stubborn concrete carcasses that stood stark and heavy in the wasteland. The only movement in the whole panorama was a scattering of people trudging along the road and one or two rickety trucks whipping up clouds of dust. Half-way down the winding mountain path, I stopped and bent over with my hands on my wobbly knees.

Just as I muttered "hot!", breathing hard, a sharp pain shot up my spine. I had been experiencing these pains for several days. I felt extremely lethargic, and I was having trouble urinating. There were no trees or thickets, and so I had to walk around, holding my abdomen, in search of a rock big enough to hide behind. I crouched down and relieved myself. The urine was murky and amber-colored. I tried to squeeze it all out, straining my abdomen muscles, but I could still not achieve a feeling of relief. For a week and a half since the explosion I had been walking almost 20 kilometers each day through the ruins, oblivious to the danger of residual radiation. I was working all day and getting only three or four hours of sleep. It was obvious that if I kept up this pace I would soon collapse. I had become keenly aware of the limits to my strength. "It's already August 18," I murmured to myself.

Disposal of the bodies of pupils (from the school where I taught) had been completed for the most part, but now children with no visible injuries were dying. These were the children whose hands I had grasped, the children with whom I had rejoiced over our escape from injury. They each followed the same steep downhill course, developing a fever, losing hair in big handfuls, and then emitting thick blackish blood from the gums. Finally, one after another, they sputtered hysterically in the throes of fever and died. There were others who suddenly and mysteriously panicked, locking themselves up in closets. The school dormitory had been closed temporarily, and I was beginning to receive word that many of the young girls who had gone home to recuperate were also falling ill.

Injured people were dying by the hundreds in the relief stations scattered throughout Nagasaki. The dead were being collected in garbage trucks and cremated *en masse* in schoolyards and other open areas. They were dragged off the mats in the relief stations and, already stiff with rigor mortis, thrown into the back of the garbage trucks. The next patient was then carried into the station and laid down for treatment on the mat occupied only minutes before by a corpse. Trapped in these ghoulish circumstances, the injured and uninjured alike became callous if they did not die or go insane first.

I had still not focused clearly on the fact that Japan had lost the war. Even on August 15, when the voice of the Emperor – which sounded all the more sad for its slightly effeminate tone – came across the air waves announcing Japan's surrender, the tears I shed did not exactly connect with the problem of what would happen once the war was over. Dragging my feet heavily down the hillside path, I thought gloomily about wandering through the corpse-strewn streets of Nagasaki and worried about how we were going to spend the winter without our clothes, but even then I was in a kind of mental fog and lacked a keen sense of reality.

I continued my zigzag trek through the ruins, trudging slowly beside the dry river bed behind the steel works in Takenokubo and negotiating the heaps of rubble on the stone foundations where houses had once stood. The river and the roadside were still scattered with corpses. Dead for the past 10 days, these were infested with maggots now and dripping a foul liquid. Huge swarms of flies buzzed about. Wielding a towel like a mace I swatted them off my back, head and face as I passed.

I noticed the carcass of a horse amid the human remains. The exposed abdomen and rib cage were occupied by a colony of plump maggots squirming about with astounding vitality. The colony was so large that it bulged beyond the original dimensions of the horse's carcass. Why such eagerness? A sickening feeling crept up from my stomach to my throat and made me spit, but it was more than nausea. It was as though the agony of being alive had condensed to liquid form and was slowly seeping into my chest. Seeing these maggots ravaging the horse somehow transformed my sadness into a mass of bitterness that threatened to overcome me.

I quickened my gait, as though fleeing from a hidden pursuer, but came to a halt after arriving near the ruins of Chinzei Middle School (present-day Kwassui High School). At the side of the road I noticed a boy standing beside a withered pine tree about two meters in height. The vision made me stop in my tracks. The boy's legs were spread open in a running posture and his hands were thrust forward as though about to grasp something. It was the corpse of a boy frozen like a statue! Looking more closely I saw that there was a dead kitten clamped to the tree with its face turned toward the boy. Scorched and covered only in the frizzled remains of fur, the kitten had obviously jumped up onto the tree to avoid the boy's advances at the moment of the atomic bomb explosion and, without disintegrating or falling down, continued to gaze with eyes frozen forever in the direction of the boy.

The boy, cat and tree were like illustrations in an action cartoon made even more surreal by the sweltering sun and the all-pervading destruction. The pine needles and slender branches were burned off, but the characteristic pine bark remained like charred fish scales. The boy's shorts were burned to his buttocks. He had no external injuries, although his hair was frizzled and his body was hideously bloated. His skin glistened as though smeared with oil, and it was stretched so tightly that it seemed ready to burst at any moment. His feet looked like they were nailed down. It was a miracle: a boy and a cat standing delicately in the wake of a cataclysm that had been fierce enough to crush rocks and twist iron pillars like strands of taffy. Perhaps a sort of wave had formed in the blast wind and formed a perfect vacuum around the boy. In any case, the result was an apparition so bloodcurdling that it bordered on the enchanting. The summer wind was blowing. I stood there in brief, bizarre juxtaposition to the boy and the cat, the shimmering waves of heat tainted with the stench of death.

Although the majority of injured people had been interned in makeshift hospitals, many unclaimed bodies had been left to decompose in the rubble, some still wrapped in bed quilts. The whole hypocenter area was strewn with the dead. I wondered how on earth they were going to dispose of all the bodies. Would they just be left there until the sun, wind and rain reduced them to invisibility? The war was lost and finished with. It was a relief to throw off the air-raid hoods and to walk outside without fear, but what were we going to do? There were no prospects whatever for the future. The horizon was bleak. It was all I could do – and all I could think of to do – just to swing the towel and ward off the flies. The sky was blue and beautiful now, liberated from the scream of air-raid sirens, but below it was a picture of hell that seemed to stretch endlessly. The misery of the people of Nagasaki was sewn forever into the seam of these two contrasting strata.

As I gazed at the boy and the cat I was overcome once more by the urge to urinate, and so I squatted down and passed water at the roadside. I was like a dog. The sharp pain in my urinary tract made me feel as though the only thing I was capable of doing properly was breathing. I finally stood up and tore myself away from the sight of the boy.

"As long as you stand you will be a monument to the horror of war," I said to the corpse before turning away. "No, even when you decompose and not a trace of you remains, you will be a monument to war. If, just as your immortal spirit can never forget, the human race will always remember the atrocity that befell this city, you may rest in peace."

I passed by the entrance to Shiroyama Primary School, where water was shooting up in fountains from the ruptured water pipes. A fine spray wafted in the air, holding a beautiful rainbow, but it drifted down only to wet the corpses rotting on the ground and to seep into the barren soil.

After a while I arrived in the Ohashi area. I had crossed Ohashi Bridge every morning for the past three days. The concrete parapets had been stripped off by the blast and the bridge now looked like a huge cutting board. The river was filled with corpses, just as it had been yesterday. Piled one upon another down the banks and into the water, the bodies protruding from the river were dark brown in hue and glistened in the sunlight while those submerged were puffed up and ghastly white. Some were still dressed in the fragments of red, black and blue clothing, presenting a startling assortment of colors. Hundreds and hundreds of them sprawled over each other in a chaotic mass that formed a great dam of death in the river. It was a dam made from the bodies of fathers, mothers, brothers, sisters, sons and daughters.

"A human dam! A human dam!" I was nearing the limits of my endurance. My body became gripped with anger and frustration for having to endure my pain and to view helplessly this unspeakable carnage and destruction. Who on earth masterminded the atrocity of blocking a river with human corpses? People were saying with sighs of relief that the war was over and that the world was at peace. But could they sit back and say calmly that this human dam was a fair price to pay for it – that war, bloodshed and human dams are inevitable?

I stood on the great slab of naked concrete that had once been a bridge and stared down at the corpses in the rippling river water, feeling the flies swarming around my back, my head, my whole body…

Remembering for 25 Years
— The Heat Rays that Burned a 16-year-old Back —

Sumiteru Taniguchi

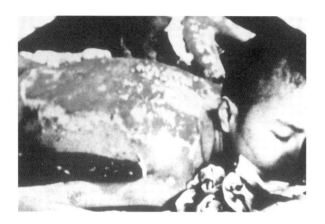

Sumiteru Taniguchi in 1946

Everyone suffers from personal grief or pain or worry, but there are some people who live without noticing this fact. There is a particularly large number of people who are unaware of the horror of war. On the occasion of the 25th anniversary of the Hiroshima and Nagasaki atomic bombings, I pick up the pen to write this account in the hope that it will help as many people as possible to understand the horror and tragedy of war and the sufferings of the atomic bomb survivors.

In 1945, I was 16 years old and working as a delivery assistant at the Moto-Hakata Post Office in Nagasaki. Although scheduled to work on the night shift on August 9, I was asked by a fellow worker to trade positions and so ended up working on the day shift. I would later suffer deep regret about this decision, lamenting the fact that I would not have encountered the atomic bombing or suffered injuries if I had stayed on the night shift.

At 11:02 a.m., I was delivering mail on a bicycle at a point 1.8 km from the hypocenter. The air-raid alarm had been lifted. In a flashing instant, I was blown off the bicycle and slapped against the ground. As I lay there with my face down, the earth seemed to shiver as in an earthquake. When I glanced upward I saw a brilliant flash of light and a child of three or four years of age swept away like a fleck of dust. A stone of about 30 centimeters in diameter hit me on a part of my lower back that would swell up two or three months later and cause me great pain. During the brief period of two or three minutes that I lay sprawled on the ground, the first thing that came to my mind was a feeling of abhorrence for war. I encouraged myself, saying, "You can't die here."

When I stood up I saw that my bicycle had been blown some three meters away and that it was now bent out of shape like taffy. If it had been functional I would probably have used it to flee. I gathered together the pieces of mail that had been scattered about, returned them to the bag and placed this beside the bicycle. It was then that I noticed my left arm. The skin from the shoulder to the fingertips had peeled off and was hanging down like a tattered rag. My right hand and left leg were burned black, and when I passed my hand around to my back I found that the clothes I had been wearing were gone and that the skin was greasy to the touch.

After that I began walking toward the mountainside. Some of the houses in the area had been completely destroyed; others were leaning over. Fires were beginning to break out. Injured people were running about crying for help. Their hair was gone, their faces and limbs were burned and swollen and blood was streaming from their wounds. I found my way to the tunnel shelter in a factory about 150 meters away and took a seat on a worktable of about one meter in height.

The tunnel was teeming with injured people and factory employees. The medicine stored in the shelter had already been exhausted. Someone used machine oil to treat the burns on my back and then cut off the skin dangling from my arm. I was lucky in that I did not shed a single drop of blood.

Soon people began to say that we could not remain in the shelter because it was part of a factory and therefore might be attacked. But I had used up all my energy just to get here and sit down, and I could not find the strength to stand up again. An uninjured person took me on his back and carried me to the hillside about 50 meters away. I lay face down on a patch of grass. There were many people here begging for water or crying for relatives as they took their last breath.

It rained that night, and I fought off death by drinking the rainwater dripping from nearby bamboo leaves.

The city was burning in the distance, the fire consuming both houses and the hillside forests and illuminating the sky like a midnight sun. Airplanes flew over, spraying the ground with machine-gun fire and whipping up screams of fear among the injured. I cannot describe the feeling of dread that came over me when bullets hit the rock face and dropped into the bushes near me.

After a night in the company of the dead, I watched the sun begin to shine brightly. I was desperately hungry and thirsty but no one gave me anything to eat or drink. I noticed a half-demolished house right below me at the foot of the hillside and decided to go there, pulling myself up with the help of the bamboo trees beside me. But I fell over, and the stem of a cut bamboo stabbed my thigh. I had to crawl out of the bushes and descend the hill to the house on my hands and knees. I removed the lid of a cistern and found that it was filled with water, and so I was able to gulp down about two liters of water and to quench my terrible thirst. Since the house could topple over at any time, I crawled out to the shade of a tree to wait for help. But the passersby were all searching for their own relatives and paid no attention to me.

On the morning of the third day, members of a rescue team finally arrived and carried me on a broken door to the relief station at Michino'o Railroad Station, a distance of about one kilometer. I stopped at Michino'o Post Office along the way, asked the employees there to contact my superiors and borrowed some clothing. I also ate some rice for the first time, and waited in the shade of the building for the train to arrive. After a while my grandfather came looking for me, and he joined me on the train to Isahaya and escorted me to the school in the city where I was admitted for treatment.

The makeshift beds in the school were just straw mats placed on the wooden floor, and I greeted the end of the war here without receiving any medication or treatment. The people working here fled to air-raid shelters whenever an airplane flew overhead, but like all the other patients I could not move. Every time someone helped me to the toilet, huge amounts of blood would well up in my wounds. This was the first time that I bled after the atomic bombing.

It was here that I heard the news that a new weapon called an "atomic bomb" had been dropped on Nagasaki and that the entire city had been destroyed. It seemed pointless to remain where I was, and so I decided to go to the village of Nagayo where relatives of my grandfather lived. I was carried to Isahaya Station by cart and boarded the train to Nagayo Station. By coincidence my relatives were at the station just when we arrived, and they took me to the school in Nagayo by cart because a navy doctor was treating the injured there. But there was no medicine available here either. All the doctor could do was smear oil mixed with paper ashes on my burns.

After that my relatives, people who I had never met before, brought meals for me everyday and gave me glutinous *mochi* rice porridge because they had heard that it was good for burns. I remember these events and all the favors I received as if they happened only yesterday.

As it turned out I was unable to receive anything like medical treatment at the makeshift hospital at Nagayo Primary School. In the middle of September my relatives carried me to Shinkozen Primary School in Nagasaki, where the Nagasaki Medical College Hospital had been temporarily re-established. It was an ordeal to ride the cart along the bumpy path to Nagasaki, a distance of more than ten kilometers. Tatami mats had been placed on the wooden floor of classrooms. I was given bedding here for the first time, but it was excruciating to have to lie constantly face down. My burns were not healing and my energy was low, but still I did not miss a single meal.

The American occupation forces arrived in Nagasaki around this time. Every day the dead were carried out into the schoolyard and other open places for cremation, and the smell drifted into the classrooms. At night I could hear the noise of cows and pigs being carried into the city by truck. The doctors tried unsuccessfully to give me blood transfusions, and I ate raw cow liver because someone suggested that it was a good way to bolster the blood.

On November 1, I was carried to the naval hospital in Omura (present-day Omura National Hospital), and when they pulled up the tatami mat upon which I had been lying, the wooden floor below was rotten and a hole of about 50 cm in diameter had opened up in it.

In Omura I again had to lie face down and motionless in bed. The doctors tried various medicines on my burns but nothing seemed to work. Although it had some effect at first, even the penicillin they gave me did little to improve my condition. From around the time of my transfer to Omura, the burns began to cause me terrible pain. The greatest ordeal of all was having my bandages changed. It is impossible to express in words the agony of lying face down day after day without any respite. It was an ordeal just to be alive, and everyday I shouted, "Kill me!" The hospital staff made sure not to place scissors or other instruments in my reach, because they knew that I would probably try to kill myself.

I slept under a mosquito net in the summer, but flies managed to get in through the smallest spaces. When I felt an irritating sensation I asked the nurses to look, and they found that maggots had formed in my burned flesh. I fell into a coma three times, and on one occasion choked and could not breathe. There was nothing that anyone could do to help me.

At the end of 1946, a new type of medicine became available, and after taking this my blood count returned to a level close to normal and my burns began to heal. In May 1947 I was finally able to sit up, and everyone (not just me) applauded this event with as much joy and enthusiasm as they would when a baby first sits up. After that the burns continued to heal and I was able to stand up and walk around.

In 1948 I underwent an operation on my left arm, but this unfortunately was not successful. To this day I cannot raise my arm beyond an angle of about 110 degrees.

At the end of March 1949 I was finally able to leave the hospital. This was a source of both joy and grief. Although happy to be leaving the hospital, I was deeply anxious about whether I would be able to hold a normal job and about the reaction of people when they saw my disfigured body. These thoughts filled me with sorrow and hatred toward war and night after night before leaving the hospital I went outside the ward and cried.

Although my burns were still not completely healed, I left Omura Hospital on March 20, 1949 and fortunately was able to return to my original workplace on April 1. In October 1951 I underwent plastic surgery on the left side of my face. The entire back of my body had been burned, and I had suffered severe bedsores on my chest, left cheek and jaw.

The burns on my back continued to refuse to heal, and I had to take many days off work. I visited every hospital I could find, only to be told each time that surgery would not help. The pain was so bad that I admitted myself to the Nagasaki Atomic Bomb Hospital and underwent surgery under general anesthesia. The results of this operation were good, and I no longer experience pain. I still remember how, when I asked if surgery would help me to raise my arm, I was told that there could be no guarantee that one or two operations would solve the problem.

In 1961 I accepted an invitation to undergo surgery in East Germany, thinking of this as a last resort. A detailed examination at the hospital in East Germany revealed that I was suffering from a chronic hematogenetic disorder and that conservative treatment, not surgery, was essential. I was so insistent on surgery that they promised to consider the possibility, but I decided against it and returned to Japan. At present I am not suffering from any significant ailment, but I tire easily and so regularly drink nutritive supplements.

What remains branded in my memory more vividly than anything else now is the tragedy of war, the carnage and suffering caused by the atomic bombing, my grandfather who attended to me for more than two years, and the doctors and nurses who helped me recover. No amount of money can buy human love, the loftiest thing of all.

I married in 1956, and until my children were born I spent many sleepless nights worrying about whether they would be healthy. Fortunately, my worry was unnecessary and I am now the father of two children.

For many years, I wore a short-sleeve shirt when I went swimming in the summer, partly because my skin was vulnerable to sunlight but also because it was painful to expose my scars to other people. But now I swim in just a bathing suit without any reservations. My skin has become more resilient, and also I hope that the shock of my appearance will help people to understand the horror of the atomic bombing.

The road ahead is still paved with thorns. In order to travel over this road, it is imperative that people join hands and work together to create a happy society free from the threat of war. I would like everyone to realize that human beings, and a spirit of humanity, must rule in human society.

Excerpt from *Mo Iya Da* ("Never Again"), Vol. 2

Fifty Years from the End of World War II : My Experience of the Atomic Bombing

Etsuko Nagano

Etsuko Nagano (second from the right) in 1943

(Ms. Nagano was exposed to the atomic bombing while working as a mobilized student in a temporary factory at the Nagasaki University Faculty of Economics in Katafuchi-machi (2.8 km from the hypocenter). She met her father and, the following day, was rejoined with her badly burned brother near her house in Zenza-machi. She also met her mother and sister, but...)

Meeting My Father in the Chaos on Inasa Bridge

On August 9, 1945, the explosion of an atomic bomb devastated the city of Nagasaki and killed an enormous number of people including my brother and sister. As a survivor of that calamity, I want to inform people everywhere about the horror of war.

The atomic bomb exploded over Nagasaki at 11:02 a.m. on August 9, 1945. I was 16 years old at the time.

It was a hot summer day and the sun was shining brightly. I had received a ration of new white running shoes, but they were so precious that I wanted to keep them unsoiled, so I left home wearing a pair of old wooden clogs. I was working at the time as a mobilized student, helping to make airplane parts in a temporary factory of the Mitsubishi Electric Plant set up in the gymnasium at the Nagasaki University Faculty of Economics, a distance of about 2.8 km from the atomic bomb hypocenter.

On the morning of August 9, an air-raid alarm was sounded but soon lifted. I departed for work as usual, leaving my mother and younger brother and sister at home. Around 11 o'clock, the windows of the factory lit up brightly, then suddenly everything seemed to go dark and the area echoed with the crash of breaking glass and the noise of falling objects. My first thought was that incendiary bombs had been dropped nearby. The blast wind soon rushed in through the broken windows, and I threw myself on the floor, covering my ears with my thumbs and my eyes with the other four fingers.

The dust was so thick that it ground between my teeth and I could not open my eyes. After a while I ran from the building, still having no idea what had happened, and fled to a nearby air-raid shelter.

One of the male workers from the factory called my name and said, "The whole Urakami district has been destroyed. Your house may have burned as well. Go home at once." I left the shelter and hurried toward the Urakami neighborhood. The damage in the Katafuchi-machi neighborhood was confined to broken windows and smashed roof tiles and so I could hardly believe what I had heard about the destruction in the Urakami area. But by the time I reached Nagasaki Station I realized that the rumors had been true: the devastation extending north from the station was evident at a glance.

The rows of houses were all demolished, and flames were spurting up here and there in the ruins. It was impossible to discern even the lines of former streets. I was so shocked that I could not decide what to do next. I had to muster up all my strength to find my way to the train tracks and to walk north to Takara-machi, the site of the second bus stop after Nagasaki Station. My house was located about ten minutes on foot to the east of the bus stop, a distance of 1.2 km from the hypocenter.

The road was gone, and I could not proceed because of the fires in the ruins. I had no choice but to take a detour to the left across Inasa Bridge and to try to get home from there.

I met my uncle by chance on the bridge, and he told me to wait because my father would be coming along soon. I strained my eyes with all my might to find my father among the people rushing back and forth across the bridge. After a while he appeared and we embraced each other, crying and rejoicing over our survival. That memory is still branded vividly in my memory. We wiped away our tears and set off along the bank of the Urakami River, determined to find the other members of our family.

On the bridge spanning the river at Mori-machi I saw the blackened corpse of a horse, still standing. Along the way I also saw a terribly burned mother with a baby still strapped to her back, sprawled dead over a sink in the ruins of a house.

Now there were hundreds of corpses scattered about, injured people who had apparently fled from the Urakami area only to die here. I too felt only half alive. Survivors bloated with burns, or naked except for patches of torn clothing stuck to their wounds, trudged by left and right. There were also countless numbers of corpses piled up along the banks of the river.

The injured cried out to us as we passed, begging for assistance or for a drink of water, but there was nothing that either my father or I could do for them. Everywhere we turned we saw people who had died under the ruins of their homes, people who had died with their arms still sticking out in a gesture of pleading for life, and injured people trudging through the wasteland like ghosts.

The neighborhoods were still hot and smoldering, making it impossible to reach our house, and so we took refuge for the time being in an air-raid shelter. I longed to see my mother and siblings, but I considered myself lucky to have been reunited with my father and thanked God for my good fortune. Still today, I cringe at the thought of what it would have been like if I had been forced to find my way through the wasteland alone.

Needless to say, there was no electricity nor any candles in the air-raid shelter. During the night, one and then another injured person passed away in the darkness. They all died in throes of pain, crying for water or mumbling their names and addresses and begging others to contact relatives. In the middle of the night I listened, trembling, to the sound of airplanes flying overhead. The tremendous "thud" "thud" of explosions echoed in the darkness, perhaps the sound of the gas tanks in Yachiyo-machi detonating in the heat.

I cannot find enough words to describe the horror of these experiences that are branded, probably for all eternity, in my brain. To this day I believe that the expression "hell on earth" applies precisely to the situation in Nagasaki on the day of the atomic bombing.

The following day the ground was still scorched and hot, but my father and I walked through the wasteland and managed to approach the area where our house had been. The first thing that caught my eye there was the blackened corpse of an adult lying near the smoldering ruins of our house. Assuming that it was my mother, I ran to the corpse and bent over it crying "Mother! Mother!"

Then a childhood friend of mine who happened by called my name and informed me that my brother had suffered burns and was lying in a nearby air-raid shelter. "I'm sorry, I couldn't do anything," she said. Hearing this, my father and I hurried to the various shelters in the neighborhood, looking into each and calling "Sei-chan!" "Sei-chan!" Finally we found a child that seemed to be my brother lying at the entrance to one of the shelters. He responded when we called his name. He had suffered burns all over his body. His face was puffed up with blisters, making it impossible for him to open his eyes. Most of his clothing had been burned or blown off in the explosion, but the tag remained on the breast of his shirt and bore the words "Kanazawa Seiji, blood-type B, grade four elementary school pupil, age nine." He was so disfigured that, without this tag, we may not have been able to identify him. He had only enough strength to nod when we called his name. It filled me with grief and horror to see my brother in such a state. After a while I asked him what had happened to our mother and sister Kuniko, but he only shook his head weakly. He could not speak. I wondered how on earth he had found his way to the shelter.

I cried bitterly when I thought about how my nine-year-old brother had spent the night alone in the midst of strangers, battling with the pain of his injuries and with loneliness and thirst.

My father found a broken door in the ruins. We lifted Seiji onto this and carried him to a relief station where first aid was being conducted, encouraging him as we walked, but all that could be done for him was to spread ointment on the burned skin. His consciousness was clear, which made the sight of his suffering all the more unbearable. If I could I wanted to take his place. We lifted him onto the door again and headed back toward the shelter, only to meet my mother and sister walking dazed and exhausted through the ruins.

My mother was alive after all! Seeing her injured son, she ran to his side and cried and screamed hysterically. When she finally calmed down to some extent we were able to ask her about what had happened. It seemed that Seiji had left the house saying that he was going to catch dragonflies. My mother and sister had been trapped under the house when it collapsed, but they managed to free themselves. Kuniko had suffered a slight injury, but my mother had escaped unscathed. After pulling herself out of the debris, my mother had noticed for the first time that all of the houses in the neighborhood had been demolished, and she watched in amazement as fires started to flare up here and there. Although worried sick about Seiji, her only alternative had been to take Kuniko and to flee up the hillside to Mt. Kompira. They had spent the night there and met us after coming back down to the neighborhood.

My brother seemed relieved to be reunited with his parents and two sisters and to be able to spend the night together in the shelter. He died on August 11, the following day, whispering "I'm thirsty" and "it hurts, it hurts." It had been a short life of only nine years. But unlike so many other atomic bomb victims, he had departed for heaven in the company of his loved ones and so was at least fortunate in that respect. He had left the house to catch dragonflies because the morning air-raid alert had been lifted, and as a result he had been exposed to the flash of the atomic bomb explosion.

I cannot help but conclude that, if the air-raid alarm had been kept in force, a large number of people including my brother would have refrained from going outdoors and therefore would have survived. Only later did I learn that the scorched corpse lying beside our house was that of the man who had lived in the house next door.

We gathered the corpses of Seiji and the approximately ten other people who had died in our neighborhood and placed them in a line for cremation, then piled scraps of wood retrieved from the ruins above them and bid our relatives a final farewell.

Rescue teams came from Shimabara, Isahaya and other nearby cities and kindly prepared food for the survivors, but under the hot sun the rice spoiled quickly. The sour smell of decomposing rice, mingling with the stench of death emanating from all the corpses in the area, created an indescribably foul smell that pervaded everything. It was such a stench that, however famished I was, I could not bring the rice to my mouth. We spent the following week in the air-raid shelter beside Zenza Primary School. The "shelter" was actually just a hole dug out of the adjacent cliff, and water dripped constantly from the ceiling onto our heads and bodies, making it impossible to sleep in the strange chill of summer.

Even after all of this, we continued to believe that Japan was winning the war and that, for the sake of our country, we had to keep struggling.

A few days later, however, enemy planes scattered leaflets over the city. Although I do not remember clearly, these said something like "Japan is defeated, and the Emperor has surrendered." We scoffed at this information, calling it lies, but on August 15 (another day that I will never forget) we learned that the war was over and that Japan had indeed been defeated. We did not have a radio and so I was unable to hear the Emperor's words directly, but everyone around me including adults and children began to weep when the news arrived. "Why...? How...?" they cried, embracing each other. We had worked so hard and endured so much! So many people had died! So many soldiers had gone to die for their country on the battlefield, leaving their bereaved families to grieve! I could not hold back a torrent of tears when I thought about all the people who had died in the atomic bombing.

I could not help but think that, if only the fighting had been called off sooner, then the atomic bombs would never have been used, there would have been no need to send *kamikaze* pilots out on suicide missions, and many deaths would have been avoided.

On August 16, we left Nagasaki without trying to do anything about our house and walked all the way to my father's hometown of Obama. We walked for hours, along the way gratefully accepting presents of straw sandals and beans from people in the town of Chijiwa, and finally reached the home of relatives who took us in with great love and kindness. So many people assisted and encouraged us along the way.

Today that road is paved and buses make the trip to Obama from Nagasaki in about an hour, but for us it was an arduous journey to say the least. Even after moving to Obama, my sister hid, crying and trembling, under bed quilts whenever she heard the sound of an airplane. Telling her that the war was over and that she had no need to worry of course made no difference.

On September 10, one month after the bombing, my sister died of atomic bomb disease. She was 13 years old. All sorts of rumors had gone around after the bombing, like the claim that anyone who drank from a well on the day of the bombing would die, or that people who lost their hair and developed spots on their skin would not survive. And just as the rumors predicted, my sister began to lose her hair, to develop spots all over her body, to bleed from the gums, and to suffer bloody stools. And then finally she died in the throes of pain. A week later my mother also developed spots on her body and was admitted to Obama Hospital for about a month, but she is, thankfully, alive and well today at the age of 94.

It was said that plants and trees would not be able to grow in the atomic wasteland for a period of 70 years, but to our astonishment the buds of weeds and saplings appeared the following spring, bringing new life back to the devastated city of Nagasaki.

After that, the restoration and revitalization of Nagasaki proceeded at a fast pace, and now it is difficult even to find traces of the atomic bomb aftermath. My husband is also an atomic bomb survivor, but we have never spoken together about our experiences because they are simply too painful. To this day, I cannot watch news or movies about war without getting upset.

Only in recent years have I begun, very gradually, to speak to my grandchildren about the atomic bombing. I think we must remember that our present prosperity rests on the basis of the noble sacrifice of so many victims. I want to convey to everyone the importance of ensuring that war is never repeated.

I decided to write about the horror and brutality of the atomic bombing when I realized that the survivors are rapidly aging and that fewer and fewer are able to recount their experiences. I made this decision on the fiftieth anniversary of the bombing in the hope that even one more person will come to understand the horror of war and the value of peace.

The priest at my local temple advised me recently to air out the vault in our family grave. When I took the lid off the urns containing the ashes of my brother and sister I was astonished to find that they had turned black like charcoal. The ashes of people who die a normal death are pinkish-white in color. It shocked me to think that the rays of the atomic bomb explosion penetrated right to the marrow of people's bones, and it made me tremble in fear all over again about the prospect of atomic bomb disease.

With the exception of schools, hospitals and a few other concrete buildings, the city of Nagasaki was comprised totally of wooden houses, and so it is no wonder that the fires spread quickly.

I would like to offer prayers for the repose of the souls of the many victims and to appeal to younger generations to avoid war and to defend peace for all eternity.

Excerpt from "Peace Talks: Something We Want You to Know"

From the Ruins of Yamazato Primary School

Hideyuki Hayashi

The area around Yamazato Primary School

1. During the months before the atomic bombing

I was transferred to Yamazato Primary School, which was only 500 meters from the point over which the atomic bomb would explode, in April 1944. Food was already in short supply by this time. The schoolyard had been plowed from corner to corner to plant sweet potatoes, and every last inch of shady space behind the school buildings was planted with squashes. We also rented a rice paddy in Motohara-machi, about 300 meters from the school, and prepared this for planting with the help of fifth and sixth-grade pupils. On the day of planting, all of the teachers canceled afternoon classes and went to the rice paddy. Since there were so few male teachers, the backbreaking task of planting the rice seedlings fell for the most part on the teenage female teachers.

After the fall of Okinawa in April 1945, the air raids by American airplanes grew more and more ferocious, and our days began and ended with the wail of sirens. At the end of June, classes were suspended in schools all across Nagasaki. But even though the scourge of air raids made it impossible to conduct classes, we could not ignore the children upon whose shoulders the future of Japan rested. In a teachers' meeting, we decided to adopt a temporary system in which pupils from the first through the sixth grade gathered in community halls or private homes in each neighborhood for classes. In this way we tried to help the children maintain their studies. The more than 30 teachers made the rounds of the neighborhoods and gave lessons, but we were able to meet our own pupils only once or twice a month. We relished these brief encounters, never knowing that in a month or two we would be bidding each other an eternal farewell.

After finishing the rounds during the morning hours, the teachers returned to dig air-raid shelters. Countless cave shelters had already been gouged from the hillsides surrounding the school to the east and north, but because these were shallow we decided to dig two deep shelters that could be joined in the interior. The male teachers wielded picks and dug away at the wall of earth, developing callouses on their unskilled hands, while the female teachers carried the broken soil away in baskets. In addition to our makeshift classes and shelter digging, we had to help alleviate the food shortage by pulling weeds in the rice paddy.

2. August 9, 1945, the day of destiny

On the fateful day of the atomic bombing (August 9), several young female teachers who had stayed overnight in the school joined Vice Principal Yukio Koga in pulling weeds from around five o'clock in the morning until breakfast and then returned to the rice paddy after the air-raid alarm was lifted.　All of the other staff members, except Asa Yoshiura who remained in the teachers' office, continued the sweaty task of digging air-raid shelters.

A little before eleven o'clock, the men took a break while I climbed halfway up the cliff to measure the height of the cave.　Mr. Sakaki was at the top of the cliff above me.　The principal, Hisayoshi Mawatari, was resting outside with Mr. Nagano and Mr. Kinoshita. The women were still standing in a line conveying the loose soil out of the shelter.

Suddenly, without warning, I heard the sound of engines. Any other time my first reaction would have been to search the sky for airplanes, but this time I felt a dark premonition – in retrospect a kind of wordless warning from heaven – and leaped instantly into the shelter, which had now reached a depth of about three meters.　In an instant I passed the fork of the road between life and death.　While I clutched the face of the wall like a lizard, a hot blast of wind rushed in from behind me.　One of the women, Eiko Kubo, who had been at the entrance and escaped death by a hair's breadth, fell in behind me crying from the pain of the heat.

I do not know how long I remained crouched inside the shelter. It seemed like an immeasurably long period of time but was probably only a few minutes.

Having no knowledge whatever about the power of the atomic bomb, I looked with disbelief at the scene that confronted me outside. The summer sun shining brightly a few minutes earlier had lost its light, and the sky looked as though a rainstorm was approaching.

The women who had been carrying soil and the men who had been wiping away perspiration were scattered on the ground. They were all naked from the waist up, stripped of their clothing either by the blast wind or the intense rays of heat. The exposed limbs and faces were severely burned, the skin hanging off in sheets like rags. It was such a hideous sight that I would have fled if I had not known that they were my colleagues.

Kame Ichinose had died instantly, thrown some ten meters from where she had been working and smashed against the cliff wall. I was astonished to see that there was not a thread of clothing left on her body, even though she had been fully dressed at the time of the explosion. Toyo Kataoka and Hideko Araki were nowhere in sight. I might have been able to identify them from the corpses nearby, but it was not until much later that I heard that they had gone to use the washroom. They may have become lost among the people from the neighborhood who took refuge in the school and later died.

After a while, Vice Principal Koga came back to the school from the rice paddy with a number of young female teachers. My joy at seeing them alive dissipated quickly when I noticed the terrible burns they had suffered. They were all shivering and complaining of the cold, but there was nothing to give them to cover their bodies. Recalling that the darkroom curtain from the science laboratory had been stored in another air-raid shelter, I went to retrieve this and gave it to the teachers. But any slight touch made their red, open burns sting with pain, and their cries of anguish echoed from every direction.

I could not find Mr. Kinoshita. I assumed that he had returned to his home in Motohara-machi. (I would hear later that he died in his family's arms the following day.)

I heard someone moaning at the top of the cliff. Remembering Mr. Sakaki, I hurried up the slope and found my colleague, who had been wearing only a pair of shorts, lying there with terrible bloody burns all over his body. His eyes had been crushed and he was biting his tongue from the pain. He begged me to kill him. "Sakaki, hold on!" I said, trying to encourage him as I carried him back to the air-raid shelter but knowing that no one could survive such severe injuries. "Mr. Hayashi, please kill me," he said again and again. All I could do was cry "don't give up!" Mr. Sakaki had graduated from Chinzei Middle School in March and had been employed as an assistant teacher in April. He still had the atmosphere of a student and so was popular among the boys. He had been working for little more than three months when his young life was snuffed out by the atomic bomb.

In the air-raid shelter, Kazuko Shioyani, apparently a Buddhist practitioner, was chanting a sutra in a loud voice, her hands clasped together.

Kayo Kubokawa had been a bright and active teacher, living by herself in the Shiroyama-machi neighborhood. She was the first to die. I called her name several times, but she did not respond. Her father came searching for her from Matsuura (in northern Nagasaki Prefecture) several days later, and he went away with the ashes of his daughter in his arms, his hopes for her survival dashed.

The scenes around the school had been more than enough to shock me when I came out of the air-raid shelter. I had assumed that this was the effect of a direct strike by incendiary bombs, but looking further, I realized that not a single house remained standing in Nishi-machi across the railroad tracks, let alone in nearby Hashiguchi-machi and Ueno-machi. I wondered if Nagasaki had become the second city, three days after Hiroshima, to be destroyed by a "new-type bomb" (no one knew anything about the atomic bomb). Soon fires began to break out in Yamazato-machi near the hypocenter and in various other areas of the ruins.

I wondered what had happened to the hundreds of children enrolled at our school. Were they trapped in the fires? I could almost hear the voices of the children, crying for their mothers and fathers as the flames crept toward them through the debris, their voices mingling with the violent cracking and popping of the conflagration. I., who was always running about mischievously; M., who was not particularly bright but who worked diligently and always came forward first for various tasks; this child, that child... Images of children's faces passed painfully through my mind. I prayed that some omnipotent deity would make a hard rain pour down upon

Nagasaki.

I looked at the school building. The room beside the science laboratory on the second floor was engulfed in flames. The firefighting tools – buckets, wet mats and fire blankets – had probably been in their place in the corridor, and I wanted to extinguish the fire if I could. But the tools had been blown away by the blast, and I could not find any of them. I might have been able to do something if there had been another two or three other uninjured people to help, but in this situation I had little choice but to sit and let the fires burn.

I went to have a look at the teachers' office. The desks, chairs, bookshelves and everything else were in an indescribable state of chaos. But in midst of the debris, where there was barely a place to step, Asa Yoshiura who had been on duty was sitting in a state of shock, but uninjured. Nobu Kumahito, Iso Iwashita and kitchen worker Tora Miyahara, who had been preparing lunch from squashes grown in the school vegetable patch, also appeared, their faces stained with blood and the shine gone from their eyes.

I went back to the air-raid shelter, where everyone was pleading desperately for water. Having heard that giving water to a seriously injured person will cause an early death, I hesitated over what to do. But finally I decided to go out in search of water, unable to ignore the entreaties of my colleagues. After trying in vain to obtain water from the taps at school, I went to houses nearby to draw well water but found that all the ropes and buckets had burned. I finally found one bucket and rope intact and carried water back to the shelter.

When I gave water to the teachers, I told them to spit it out after moistening their mouths. But they ignored me, gulped the water down with great relish, and I could not stop them. Injured people from the surrounding neighborhoods gathered one after another in the school shelter. They had also suffered terrible burns; they did not even look human. Again, I could not turn my back and refuse these people's impassioned pleas for "just a sip" of water.

Two of the classrooms in our school were being used as offices for the Mitsubishi Arms Factory, the facility that had manufactured the torpedoes used in the attack on Pearl Harbor. The pretty students from Nagasaki Prefectural Girls High School, who had been mobilized to work here and who used to wear pink ribbons in their hair, had apparently been killed instantly in the explosion and their corpses carried out onto the schoolyard.

Among the more than 30 teachers and staff who had been working at the school, I was the only man to escape injury. Eiko Kubo and Kazuko Matsuzaki, who had leaped into the air-raid shelter behind me, had also escaped injury, but there was nothing that the three of us could do. I was standing in a daze in the schoolyard when someone with terrible burns on his face and limbs came up to me and asked, "Mr. Hayashi, where is the relief station?" Seeing that I did not recognize him, the injured person said, "It's me, Araki from Nishi-Urakami Primary School." Only then did I realize that I was speaking to the husband of Hideko Araki, a teacher at our school. Mr. Araki was a teacher at Nishi-Urakami Primary School.

I met him frequently on the way to work and we always exchanged greetings. And yet now he had changed so much that I had no idea who he was. I learned that he had been in a shrine in Nishi-machi as part of the dispersion of classes to venues around the neighborhood. He collapsed in the air-raid shelter at Yamazato Primary School and was taken by colleagues to Nishi-Urakami Primary School two or three days later. But he also succumbed to his injuries. Mr. and Mrs. Araki, who had left their elderly parents on the island of Amakusa in Kumamoto Prefecture, devoted themselves to the wartime education of children only to perish in the atomic bombing.

The houses of most of the teachers and staff were located near the school and so were undoubtedly devastated by the explosion. Having no home to return to, many of them remained in the air-raid shelter. Harue Kitamura and Chie Kakimoto, who had been among the women who suffered burns while working in the rice paddy, later returned to their homes in the more distant neighborhood of Nameshi, but they died on August 12 and 17 respectively. Ms. Kitamura was a bright young teacher who had been employed in April after graduating from teacher's college. Ms. Kakimoto, who had been employed in June 1944, was a friendly and honorable woman who had enjoyed the affection of her colleagues for more than a year. It was a comfort at least to know that they had both been able to depart this world in the arms of their parents and loved ones.

Residents of Shiroyama-machi, Teruko Nagaoka, Teruchiyo Inoue and Sumiko Nakamura, who had also been among the women who suffered burns at the rice paddy, later returned to their homes but also died a few days later.

Although reluctant to leave my injured homeless colleagues, worry about my own family compelled me to set off toward my house in Showa-machi that evening. I braced myself for the worst. Already nerve-racked from the labor of helping the injured, I became so consumed with worry as I approached my neighborhood that I broke into a run. The house was completely destroyed, as I had feared, but, although I could not find them at first, I learned that all of my family members had survived and fled to the hillside. I could only raise my hands in a prayer of gratitude at the fact that, even though we had been so close to the hypocenter, I had miraculously escaped injury and all the members of my family were safe.

3. The deaths of my colleagues

On August 10 (the day after the atomic bombing), I went back to the air-raid shelter, my heart beating with apprehension about how many of the injured had managed to survive through the night.

Principal Mawatari and 11 others were weak but still alive. Makiko Yuri and Teruko Yamada had passed away during the night, and Ms. Yuri's father was cremating her remains when I arrived.

Seeing that the survivors had not eaten anything since lunch the previous day, I walked to nearby Ohashi, received rations of rice balls and then used a pot to boil these into a porridge that I gave to them in small amounts. Yoshiichi Nagano, who had suffered burns from his head to his face but did not utter the slightest complaint, asked for a second helping after finishing the first and ate this austere meal with obvious pleasure. The image of Mr. Nagano is branded in my memory to this day. Mr. Nagano, who had made us laugh so often with his wry jokes, later passed away as though following the members of his family, all of whom had perished in their house in Yamazato-machi.

I wanted to treat the burns of the injured with ointment but none was available. No medical team had come to the area yet. In response to a request from Principal Mawatari, I made the trip to Nagasaki City Hall to report the damage suffered by our school. The area from Oka-machi to Matsuyama-machi, Hamaguchi-machi and Iwakawa-machi was a field of scorched rubble as far as the eye could see. Smoke was still curling up from the ruins, broken roof tiles covered the road and hundreds and hundreds of blackened corpses with exposed white bones lay scattered amid the debris and fallen telephone poles, emitting the pungent smell of death. Cowering in the shade of a broken wall whenever an airplane passed overhead, I made my way along the road with slow progress. In Iwakawa-machi, a military team was trying to clear obstacles from the road. I managed to reach City Hall, but no medical supplies were available there either.

Only when an army medical officer later came to inspect Yamazato Primary School was I able to insist that he provide assistance and to have him apply bandages to the injured.

On August 11 (two days after the atomic bombing), a navy medical team finally arrived at Yamazato Primary School and established a treatment unit in the concrete shell of the ruined building. The doctors and orderlies were overcome with work as one injured person after another arrived for treatment, and they had no time to come to the air-raid shelter. I was able to help some of my colleagues, grasping them by the shoulders and hobbling with them across the schoolyard to the school building about 100 meters away. And after a while the doctors finally responded to my entreaties to come to the air-raid shelter to provide treatment for the severely injured.

Ichiro Kawashita, a teacher who had been working at my school until June but had transferred to Katsuyama Primary School, appeared at the shelter and began to help me and to offer words of encouragement to the injured. Having had to deal with the situation alone up to that point, I deeply appreciated his assistance. It would have been best for the teachers and staff if their relatives came for them, but since most of them lived in the hypocenter area it was unlikely that any had survived. Moreover, there was no way to make contact. I asked Mr. Kawashita to call more teachers from other schools to provide assistance.

Vice-principal Koga's condition gradually deteriorated, and he died that night at almost the same time as Yoshiichi Nagano. Mr. Koga, who lived in Matsuyama-machi directly under the explosion point of the atomic bomb, had lost his entire family. It filled me with anguish to see Mr. Koga and my other colleagues die without a loved-one to comfort them on their deathbed.

Exhausted and half-dead myself from attending to the injured, I walked four kilometers to my parents' house in Iwaya-machi, reaching it after ten o'clock at night.

On the afternoon of August 12 (four days after the bombing), about ten teachers from various schools in Nagasaki city arrived to provide assistance. They were shocked to see the many corpses that had to be cremated. I also asked them to make boxes in which to place the ashes of the deceased. Later, relatives coming from distant places expressed gratitude for our efforts, in the midst of this terrible situation, to place the ashes in boxes.

Toshiko Yamada, another teacher, joined the list of the dead. Since she lived in Ueno-machi, it seemed likely that her family members had all been killed. No one ever came to ask for her. I remembered going to her family's loquat orchard on the hillside the previous year and filling my stomach with the delicious fruit.

It was a feeling of excruciating loneliness to watch the death toll rise day by day.

On August 13 (five days after the bombing), it was decided that the injured should be carried by truck to the neighboring community of Togitsu, where they could receive better treatment. We helped three teachers – Shizue Kaneko, Hisako Sumiyoshi and Yuko Tsurumaki – as well as the school nurse, Kimiko Yamamoto, onto the truck. Kazuko Shiotani begged to be taken with them, striving to lift herself up, but her condition seemed beyond hope. As I feared, she passed away around three o'clock.   The only member of her family to survive was a brother who had been working in a factory in Nagayo village.   He came looking for her but unfortunately did not make it in time.   It was a great disappointment for me as well.   I had walked to Nagayo that morning, dragging my blistered feet, only to hear that he had gone to Nagasaki.   It seemed that he had heard about my visit when he went back to Nagayo and that he had come to Yamazato Primary School as quickly as possible.

Principal Mawatari, who had held on to the end, finally took his last breath in the arms of his son and only surviving family member.

On August 14 (six days after the bombing) I began to worry about the four women that we sent to Togitsu for treatment.   To make the long walk there would mean developing blisters all over my feet, but the situation did not allow complaints about personal difficulties.   It took me twice as long as usual to walk to the school in Togitsu, but when I arrived there I was relieved to hear that the four were still alive.   My heart was full of regret over the fact that they had been left to lie for hours on stretchers under the hot sun at Ohashi Bridge and that, after the truck finally arrived, they had had to endure the rocky ride to Togitsu.

On August 16 (eight days after the bombing), I went to the school in Togitsu again.   My four colleagues had been in good spirits two days earlier and so I assumed that they would be on their way to recovery, but I found that Ms. Kaneko had died that morning and that Ms. Tsurumaki was also on the verge of death.   If I had known that this was going to happen, even though they had seemed well, I would never have put them through the agony of the long trip to Togitsu.   There was apparently no hope for the nurse Ms. Yamamoto either.

"I'm so sorry, I'm so sorry," I said, but no amount of apologies could help.

On my way back to Yamazato Primary School I met the father of my fellow teacher Chiyoko Hoshino and learned that she had passed away at her home on the 14th.   I remembered how her mother had come to the school looking for her and how happy and encouraged Chiyoko had been when they met.   I could still see her leaving for home. My heart grew darker and darker with each new piece of tragic news.

On August 17 (nine days after the bombing), I joined Ms. Kaneko's sister and Teruko Yanada's father in pulling a cart to Togitsu to fetch Ms. Kaneko's remains. We learned that both Ms. Yamamoto and Ms. Sumiyoshi had died that morning. Only the previous day, Ms. Sumiyoshi had been in good spirits when we spoke to each other and said goodbye. I could no longer even utter a gasp of surprise over the evanescence of human life. And at the same time, I felt a new wave of anger at the indiscriminate carnage caused by the atomic bomb.

Like our principal Mr. Mawatari, Ms. Sumiyoshi had been transferred to the school only in mid-June. They would not have been exposed to this calamity if they had never come to Yamazato Primary School. There is nothing more impossible to predict than human fate.

With Ms. Yamamoto's mother weeping nearby, we placed the corpses of Ms. Kaneko and Ms. Yamamoto on the cart and carried them down the road like luggage.

As it turned out, all of the four women we sent to Togitsu passed away.

Now the only two survivors were my fellow teacher Nobu Kumashiro and the school helper Tora Miyahara. Ms. Kumashiro had been cut by flying glass but had suffered no burns, and so I assumed that she would recover. But she followed her deceased colleagues into the arms of death on August 20, the 12th day after the atomic bombing.

Ms. Miyahara, who returned to her family home in Muramatsu Village (present-day Kinkai-cho), also took a turn for the worst. Her husband, Mantaro Miyahara, who had worked as the school janitor for many years, had been killed instantly in the explosion, his remains burning without leaving even a trace.

My fellow teacher Iso Iwashita, who had returned to her home on the coal-mining island of Takashima two days after the bombing, had seemed fine, but I heard later from her bereaved family that she had been "called to the lap of God" on September 6, making her the last of my colleagues to die.

In this way, 26 teachers including the principal Mr. Mawatari, two helpers, and between 1,000 and 2,000 pupils at Yamazato Primary School fell victim to the atomic bomb. Of the more than 30 teachers employed by the school, the only survivors were Asa Yoshiura, Kazuko Matsuzaki, Eiko Kubo and myself (who had been at the school but managed miraculously to escape serious injury) as well as Hisako Yamazaki and Taeko Kataoka, who had been on leave that day.

A nightmarish two weeks passed. After watching my injured and burned colleagues succumb one after another, I also collapsed like a puppet with its strings cut. From the beginning of September, I suffered from a high fever, a temperature of 39 degrees continuing for several days. This was a time when the people who had managed to survive began to suffer from fever, bleeding, diarrhea and other symptoms of so-called atomic bomb disease and to die one after another, and it seemed like I was going to join them. But I resisted with all my might and strove to stay alive.

After about two weeks, although still feeling weak, I was able to get up. I was worried about the school and wanted to report for work as soon as possible, but my body would not listen. Hisako Yamazaki and Taeko Kataoka came to visit me, and I was relieved to hear from them that Shigeaki Harada (former principal of Yamazato Primary School and now principal of Oura Primary School) and Ichibe Kawashita (who had been transferred to Katsuyama Primary School in June), had been assigned to manage the ruins of Yamazato Primary School because of their knowledge of the school.

On September 14, I was feeling rather well and so lifted myself out of bed and went to receive a blood test at Shinkozen Primary School, which was serving at the time as a temporary atomic bomb relief hospital. The results showed that my white blood cell count was little more than 3,000, or about half that of a healthy person. I did not have the money to purchase a train ticket, and the streetcars were still out of operation, and so I had no choice but to walk to my home about eight kilometers away.

On September 19, a service was held at Kotaiji Temple in Tera-machi to pray for the repose of the more than 70 staff members and 3,000 pupils of Nagasaki primary schools who had fallen victim to the atomic bombing. I could only raise my hands in prayer and say, "Rest in peace."

Most of these victims had been exposed to the explosion at Yamazato Primary School and Shiroyama Primary School, the schools closest to the hypocenter.

4. Taking steps to rebuild Yamazato Primary School

A month after the atomic bombing we had to consider ways to reopen our school. The concrete building of Yamazato Primary School had withstood the blast and stood as a noble symbol of the ordeal of the Urakami valley. But now only the outer shell remained; the interior had burned completely and the window frames were twisted out of shape and covered with rust.

The pillars of the school administration, including the principal, vice-principal, 28 teachers and helpers, had perished in the bombing. What was left for the two young women teachers and me to do? We did not even know how many pupils had survived. The operation of Yamazato Primary School was in a state of complete paralysis.

In any case, our first task was to determine the names and whereabouts of the surviving pupils and to somehow bring them together. We put up posters announcing the reopening of the school at various locations in the wasteland and, on September 20, held an assembly on the grounds of Nagasaki Teachers College in Nishi-Urakami. About 100 pupils gathered, mostly children living in Ieno-machi, Motohara-machi and other neighborhoods relatively distant from the hypocenter.

We decided to resume classes in the concrete skeleton of Yamazato Primary School and, with the help of the surviving pupils, began the work of cleaning out and rearranging the devastated classrooms. Understandably, our progress was very slow. It was a heavy burden for these small children who had lost their homes and their families and had so little reason to travail. The two teachers Isao Iwanaga and Satoshi Oishi, who had returned to Nagasaki from military service, worked with great assiduousness and in that way encouraged the children to look to the future.

The schoolyard was still strewn with bones and no one wanted to dispose of them. Winter was approaching, but we had neither wooden floors beneath our feet nor windowpanes to block the wind and so could hardly expect to conduct classes. We had no choice but to borrow classrooms at the Nagasaki Teachers College about one kilometer away. (The concrete building was still standing but the wooden buildings had all burned to the ground, and as a result the college had been moved to Omura City, Nishi-Urakami Primary School moving into the concrete building.)

For several days, the smaller children carried the chairs that had escaped the fires while the older children carried desks from the ruins of Yamazato Primary School. The three classrooms allotted for our use were filled with the heavy metal cylinders of torpedoes left behind by the Mitsubishi Arms Factory, which had set up a temporary plant there. Before finally beginning classes on November 9, we had to carry these outside, and we used strips of wood to cover the windows and fend off the cold of winter. A semester and a half had already passed, and at first we were able to conduct only about one-third of the normal curriculum in the semi-darkness of these makeshift classrooms.

The classrooms, however dismal, thus became available, but none of the children had books, notebooks or pencils. I managed to obtain a few books from the school of my previous posting in Inasa and to scrape together some paper and pencils, but the classes could only be conducted by copying the books, with several children crowding around each desk.

Other children who had heard the news of the reopening began to arrive, one today, two tomorrow, and by this time the enrolment had rebounded to over 300. When they appeared, we gathered around these children with cheers of welcome and congratulated them on their survival.

At first there had been only 20 sixth grade pupils, but the

number soon grew to 75, causing a shortage of desks and chairs and making it necessary to return repeatedly to Yamazato Primary School to fetch broken furniture.

On March 23 the following year, we conducted a graduation ceremony and brought a year of tragedy and turbulence to a close. At the same time the previous year, the wall at the front of the school had been decorated with a curtain, the national flag had flown prominently, the school flag and beautifully arranged flowers had been on display, dignified guests had come to mark the occasion, and the ceremony room had been filled with mothers, fathers and relatives. But this year, there were no guests, nor even any mothers or fathers, the people who would have been more happy and proud than anyone to greet this day. A single flower placed in a small vase was the only comfort and the only reminder of the significance of this occasion. And when the usual songs were sung, they were punctuated with sobs and dampened with tears.

The graduating children had seen only hardships: constant air-raid alarms, the atomic bombing, untold difficulties in the aftermath and altogether unsatisfactory classes. I was filled with a feeling of remorse. Off they went, embracing hopes for a higher education while having to bear the burden of caring for their siblings and to struggle to find a place in the chaos of society. I prayed with all my heart for their divine protection.

5. Our task now

High-rise buildings now compete for space on the former atomic wasteland in the Urakami area, and there is little to serve as a reminder of the atomic bombing. Peace Park and Hypocenter Park are now popular sightseeing spots visited daily by groups of tourists and children on school excursions. And it is understandable that few of these people can even imagine the devastation of yesteryear.

Japan is the only country in the world to have suffered the destruction of nuclear weapons, but most Japanese people look upon the atomic bombings as idle spectators, and even the residents of

Nagasaki Prefecture who were not directly exposed have little appreciation for the horror of the atomic bomb experience. With the passage of several decades, the feelings of trepidation and abomination can only grow faint.

Moreover, the events of that time were so horrific that many people prefer not to even think about the atomic bombing and its aftermath. Sometimes I am also overcome with thoughts like this, but in order to ensure that this disaster is never repeated, the atomic bomb survivors must not remain silent. To speak and to inform is our greatest duty toward the tens of thousands of people who perished in the atomic bombing.

Excerpt from *Mo Iya Da* ("Never Again"), Vol. 2

From a Diary Before and After
the Atomic Bombing

Atsuyuki Matsuo

The Atsuyuki Matsuo Monument

The following are excerpts from a diary centering around the Nagasaki atomic bombing. I hope that it will help the reader imagine the plight of a family destroyed by the explosion of an atomic bomb.

24 January 1945

It is a truly beautiful snowfall. The snow on rooftops and on the mountains surrounding the city shines wondrously in the winter sunlight.

> Seeing the light
> And the dripping snow
> I think, Shall I name the baby "Yukiko" (snow child)?

Finally we did decide on the name Yukiko. This also borrowed the word "yuki" from my name. The baby sleeps peacefully, her face still red from birth.

15 February 1945

My eldest son Umito's entrance examination is approaching. I hope he gets into the school without any trouble. On top of all the irritating worries in our personal lives, the war is taking a very bad turn for the worse. The future is dark for our forces in the Philippines; the enemy has already entered Manila. We can no longer scoff at the possibility of our main islands being invaded. Rumors are going around that we may have to hand over a portion of Kyushu Island to the invading armies. Yet despite all the worries bothering me day and night, I am very grateful that Michiko and her siblings are healthy and happy. I am very, very grateful.

9 August 1945 (the diary is written hereafter in the past tense)

It was a beautiful clear day, and so hot that I wore only an undershirt at the office. I had been on duty the night before, but my wife had called me in the evening to ask if I would come home for dinner. "We have been instructed to stay here from today onwards," I had replied. It seems that the air raid on Hiroshima caused severe damage. Please be on guard." I added the last part as a kind of warning."

My fellow worker Wataya decided to go out for lunch in Kabashima-machi. I ascended the stairs to the second floor only to hear the last part of a radio announcement: "... flying west over Shimabara Peninsula." Musing that Kumamoto, Shimabara, and Nagasaki run in one straight line from east to west, I said to everyone as I entered the office: "If planes are flying west over Shimabara then they must be on their way to Nagasaki." Before I could reach my desk the bell that warns of the approach of enemy airplanes began to ring, even though the air-raid sirens remained silent (the air-raid alarm had been lifted about 9:30 that morning). In the short span of a second or two, I heard the distant drone of airplanes and stood up to don my jacket, intending to place documents in an emergency bag. Suddenly a brilliant yellow light enveloped everything. At the same time a tempestuous gust of hot air blew in through the conference room from the direction of Ohato, and a thunderous "boom!" shook the earth. Someone shouted "Get down!" and I joined the others in hitting the floor, but the blast wind rocked the whole building and smashed the windows and window frames in a violent avalanche of sound. After waiting for the rocking to stop, lying prone under our desks, we shouted frantically to each other, "Let's get out!" We tried to descend the emergency staircase but a broken door blocked the way. We headed back to take the other stairs, but it was treacherous because the floor was strewn with jagged splinters of wood and glass. Because of athlete's foot I was wearing only thin sandals and so it was extremely difficult to walk. The air was choked with black smoke. We fled as fast as we could to the air-raid shelter, noticing that many among us had been injured by flying glass.

We gave first-aid treatment to the wounded in the shelter. The worst injuries were caused by glass splinters in the buttocks, but soon people from the processing plant and warehouse began to come into the shelter, and some of them had suffered burns. They went to receive treatment in the air-raid shelter at the army hospital next door. The warning bell was still ringing and so we hesitated to go outdoors. Fires were breaking out and spreading around Nagasaki Station and the Ohato area. Finding an opportunity to leave the shelter, I walked up the path to the nearby elevation where Kwassui Women's College stands and looked out over the city. Raging fires and thick smoke were visible as far as the arms factory in Mori-machi, but the area beyond that was completely hidden from view. I was overcome with worry about my daughter Michiko, who was working at the time in the arms factory. I suspected that fires were burning near our home in Shiroyama-machi as well, but there was no information available about that part of the city.

At about four o'clock in the afternoon, I learned that security forces were going to carry a load of biscuits to the Prefectural Girls High School, and out of some sort of presentiment, I volunteered to help. The fires were spreading furiously, already consuming the Prefectural Government Building. When I arrived at the girls school I was informed by the warehouse guard, Mr. Fukagawa, that Michiko was injured and interned in the school. Shocked yet joyful, I was directed by a teacher to the Tachibana dormitory and I found Michiko there with burns on her face and arms. She was up, though, and able to walk. Tears flowed from my eyes. There were five or six other girls with her.

I wanted to let the other members of our family in Shiroyama-machi know that Michiko was safe. I decided to take the mountain pass from Nishiyama reservoir over to the Urakami Theological Seminary. It was probably about seven o'clock in the evening when I set out.

It was pitch dark by the time I reached the pass, and I began to meet groups of injured people coming the other way. I could see the crushed or burned ruins of farmers' houses silhouetted in the darkness. There were no signs of human life near them. From time to time as I walked, someone would call out, "Who is it?" and when I said, "Just a passerby," the person would become silent. I wondered why they asked such a question.

When I arrived in the city below I found trees lying on the

streets and telephone wires scattered all around. The embers of the gutted Urakami Theological Seminary were still glowing. The scale of the destruction surpassed my worst fears. The ground was so hot that I could go neither forward nor back. I jumped into a field from the road leading to Urakami Cathedral and made my way as best I could along the edge of the fields. The arms factory appeared to my right, now in a shocking state of ruin. Nothing remained of the vegetables that had been growing in the fields.

I heard the sound of an approaching airplane. As I ducked into an indentation in the field a bomb exploded over the burning arms factory and for a moment illuminated the area. It did not generate a blast like the bomb this morning, however, and so I assumed that it had been an incendiary bomb. I was amazed at the enemy's persistence in bombing places that were already on fire.

In the middle of a field where the gate to the industrial school had been, I met a group of four or five people lying on the ground, apparently staying the night there, and again I was asked: "Who are you?"

"I'm trying to return to Shiroyama-machi but I can't find the way," I answered.

"Go down to the Urakami River and cross it," one of the people suggested. "Then head back along the other bank. You'll make better headway if you go over the places where the vegetable plots used to be."

Heeding this advice, I decided to pass between Yamazato Elementary School and the prison and to go down to the river. The school was still in flames. The crackling sound was probably the rice reserves burning. From the shadows of a nearby field I heard the voice of someone begging for water, and I began to realize more clearly the horror of what had happened.

I crossed the Urakami River and then, crossing back again at Ohashi Bridge, made my way toward Shiroyama-machi along the bank of the river. It was very dark and so I could not see well, but nothing visible had escaped destruction. The municipal commercial school was in flames. The artificial river embankment had crumbled and huge blocks of concrete barred the way.

I arrived at last in Shiroyama-machi but the whole area was a scorched field of rubble; I could not even discern which road led to my house. As I stood there dumbfounded, Mr. Wakita, a section chief at the Food Supply Headquarters where I worked, came along by chance. He had gone to the site of his house but had found nothing but a pile of ashes. His wife had been ill and so was probably killed in the fire. He was on his way back to the office, having abandoned all hope for her survival. As I listened to his story, the dark premonition that my family had also been killed stabbed my heart. We separated there, and I hurried along a clearing that I thought would lead to my house. The time was probably about 10:00 p.m.

The Shiroyama main street, which had been such a familiar sight to me, was now part of the gutted wasteland and utterly unrecognizable. I managed to find the stone stairwell leading up to our house, but the trees in Yasaka Shinto Shrine had vanished and so my disorientation only continued. I finally arrived at the site of our house. Amazingly enough, a group of four or five houses including our own had been demolished by the explosion but had escaped the ensuing fires, even though the entire surrounding area had been reduced to ashes. I stood on the road and gazed in mortification at our house, now a chaotic pile of lumber. I cringed at the thought that my wife and children were perhaps lying beneath it. I moved towards the house, stepping over the pillars and beams scattered wildly about the yard, and called out the names of my wife and children. There was no response.

I went and asked the few remaining people in the area if they knew anything about my family's whereabouts. But the answer was no, and so I went back to the house once more.

Listening carefully I heard the faint sound of a voice. I shouted "I'm coming!" and turned in the direction of the voice, which I soon realized was coming from the ruins of the Koga family's house next door. "Please lift away this beam," said the voice feebly when I approached. I tried with all my might to lift the beam but every time I moved it a deluge of soil and broken roof tiles rushed in onto the trapped person. It seemed to be Mr. Koga's wife, and near her I could also hear the voice of a little girl begging for help. I tried again and

131

again but it was no use. I asked another neighbor to help but he said it was too dangerous in the dark and suggested that we wait until dawn and then go with several others. (We rescued the mother and child the following day but they both died later.)

I decided to wait until dawn to dig out my wife and children too, and I went to the cave shelter in our garden, planning to spend the rest of the night inside it. When I crawled in, though, my hand touched the cold foot of a human being. "Who is it?" I blurted in surprise. "Umito," came the voice of my eldest son. It is impossible to describe the joy I felt at knowing he was alive.

"I was sitting out on the verandah doing some work when the bomb exploded," Umito explained. "I was pinned under the debris of the house but managed to crawl out. I searched for mother but couldn't find her and I came in here to sleep.

"Are you injured?" I asked.

"I've got some burns, but they're not serious," he replied. "Chihara (a neighborhood friend) and I ate some pears and canned sardines that were in here, but I think they were spoiled because we vomited and got diarrhea."

"It's pitch dark and enemy planes are flying over, so let's wait until dawn," I said, suggesting that we sleep inside the shelter. "Your wounds are light and Michiko is safe in Yanohira-machi. The three of us have to do our very best. Your mother died with Hiroto and Yukiko, and I know that she would want us to carry on now." During the night Umito had several bouts of diarrhea and I helped him out of the shelter each time. The mountains were smoldering with fire and the whole area was a desolate wasteland. I thought about the transitory lives of my wife Chiyoko and my children Hiroto and Yukiko, and, exhausted but unable to sleep, spent the rest of the night in a kind of stupor.

10 August 1945

When the light of morning began to color the sky, I emerged from the shelter and from a sleepless night to look around. The entire three-kilometer space of land stretching from the mountains on the east to those on the west was flattened, and everything including trees and the tiered mountain vegetable fields was reduced to ashes. This indescribably desolate and miserable vision unfolded before me as far as the eye could see. There was also a strange mist hanging in the air, different from anything I had ever seen before. Umito's burns were severe. They spread over half his back and the rear side of both arms. I wanted to get medical treatment for him, but it was unlikely that a rescue team would come yet. In the distance I could see a few members of the Obama Volunteer Corps, men and women wearing *happi* coats, and I shouted to them and ask them to come. I carried Umito out of the shelter after their arrival, and they scooped a white liquid from a bucket and spread it over his burns with a brush, picking away the dangling skin as they did. The large extent of the burns worried me very much.

Someone walking by on the road beside the house said, "Your wife is just down the street." Almost jumping up and dancing with joy, I immediately ran off to look for her. I found her near the road leading out to the right from Yasaka Shrine, no more than 20 meters away from where Umito was. She had been only a stone's throw from the house, but lacked the strength even to make her way back. Chiyoko was lying in the middle of a field on a tatami mat provided by a family who had also fled to the field, and lying beside her were the tiny corpses of Hiroto and Yukiko. It was a crushing blow to see them. Chiyoko had burns on her face, arms and legs. Four year-old Hiroto had no serious wounds, but apparently he had developed brain fever soon after the explosion. He had sucked on a stick and said, "This is sugar cane. It's good." It seems that he had lost his wooden clogs in the chaos and that it troubled him very much. He had spoken from time to time, saying things like, "Was that an air raid?" but his condition had gradually worsened and he died struggling that evening. One year-old Yukiko had been in good spirits despite the deep wound on her forehead, and sucked milk from her mother's breasts, but she died suddenly that morning as well.

I carried Chiyoko into the shelter, then laid the corpses of the children in the yard and covered them with a piece of cloth. It was an agony to have to leave the two of them lying there on the ground. The hot summer sun was beating down and flies were swarming about.

Chiyoko also had diarrhea. There was neither emergency food distribution nor any kind of relief. The injured were simply left to die. An announcement came from somewhere that rice porridge would be served. I went to the place in our neighborhood where it was being cooked and received a small amount. The only utensil we had was a dipper without a handle, and so I used it to receive the porridge and to feed Chiyoko and Umito. Both of them were unbearably thirsty.

Around noon Umito started to get chills. He seemed to have a fever and to be experiencing great discomfort. Unable to remain still, he would sit up but then have to lie down again, repeating the cycle over and over. His burns seemed to be causing him great agony, so I took the little oil we had left and spread it over the wounds. I also applied talcum powder I found in a cosmetics box owned by the Koga family. His brain became affected by the fever and he began to mumble things about his work at school, all the time moving his fingers in a rhythmical way as though tapping something. His legs began to turn cold and I tried to warm them up by rubbing them, but a feeling of hopelessness came over me. I went to draw some water but when I returned I found him lying face down and dead, having crawled out to where his mother was lying. (Umito had been in the interior of the shelter while Chiyoko was lying at the entrance.) Chiyoko told me that he had moaned, "It hurts" and crawled out toward her. She said that he seemed to be smiling, and looking in his face I saw that his expression had indeed become peaceful and relieved. This gave me some small measure of solace. He had survived the day before, and I had hoped that he might somehow manage to live. His death was and always will be a great thorn in my heart.

From the time Umito's condition worsened until he died, Chiyoko just lay where she was in a semi-comatose state. She sometimes awoke and asked me to suck the milk from her breasts because of the unbearable pain. It only filled me with grief that, even though her children were dead and she herself was nearing death, her breasts continued to produce milk. I had to leave the two small children lying out in the garden, but for tonight I wanted to be near Umito, and so I left him lying as he was at Chiyoko's side inside the shelter, and we greeted the arrival of night together. Smoke had begun to curl up from the hillsides that afternoon. Fires broke out around dusk and they burned all through the night. I could hear the crackling sound of fires at Shiroyama Elementary School. Again, it was probably the rice reserves going up in smoke. From time to time enemy airplanes flew overhead. Our neighbor Mr. Koga (who later became director of the Mitsubishi Nagasaki Shipyard) arrived home and inquired about his wife. (There were two Koga families in our neighborhood.) According to Chiyoko, Mrs. Koga had left for Matsuyama Post Office after the lifting of the morning air-raid alarm, and she was probably in that area (near the hypocenter) when the bomb exploded. I related this information to Mr. Koga. Among the thirteen housewives living in our immediate neighborhood, Chiyoko was the lone survivor and so the only witness to the events in the neighborhood at the time of the explosion. (I learned only after Chiyoko's death that the Shiraishi family had gone to Togitsu after the lifting of the alarm and so had survived.) In any case, almost all the people in this area at the time of the explosion were dead. Today I witnessed the death of my son Umito, and the grief I felt now was deeper than any I had ever imagined. Umito, Hiroto, Yukiko. My life of devotion to my children – the life I worked so hard to establish – was torn up by the roots.

11 August 1945

Chiyoko, Umito and I spent the night in the dampness of the shelter, one of us dead and one dying. My misery was boundless.

When morning came I carried Umito out of the shelter and placed him on the ground beside his brother and sister. The three corpses lay there on the ground under the rays of the hot summer sun. The pumpkin field Umito had diligently cultivated had been ravaged by the blast, and not even a leaf or piece of stem remained. The three dead bodies of my children lay side by side in an open space amid the shattered beams and broken roof tiles. A neighbor named Kino helped me carry Umito's body out of the shelter. Kino, Urakawa, Urakawa's son, Mori and Nakamura, all of whom had all been away at work at the time of the explosion, were the only survivors from our neighborhood association. In other words, all the people who had been at home in Shiroyama-machi when the bomb exploded were killed immediately or died soon after. The survivors gathered near the site of the local kindergarten, built a makeshift floor out of odd tatami mats and doors and tried to prepare food. At night we slept outside or in a ditch laid with boards. Kino had lost his wife and two children, and he wanted to stay nearby until finding their remains in the gutted family house. Our food supply consisted of rice that had been kept in the shelter in case of emergency and a few half-burnt pumpkins we found in the fields or freshly-planted potatoes we dug up. We retrieved a few dishes and pots from the ruins of the houses that had escaped the fires and used them for our austere meals.

I noticed that a relief team from the Army Hospital had finally arrived and set up camp on the hill above Shiroyama Elementary School. Instructions came to bring all the survivors in this area to the kindergarten, and so I carried Chiyoko there on my back and put her on a bed quilt to rest. The morning sun was shining brightly. I tried to give her some shade by hanging a torn mosquito net over her face. There were two other injured people waiting for treatment.

Chiyoko's injuries did not seem serious, but she was suffering from diarrhea and seemed extremely weak. I wanted the relief team to provide treatment immediately, but crowds of injured people were gathered at their camp and they had still not left on rounds. It was then that Chiyoko's mother and sister arrived.

Dressed in padded air-raid costumes, they had obviously come prepared for the worst. Enemy planes were still flying frequently over Nagasaki. They stayed for a while, then departed saying that they would visit the Maruta family in Takenokubo before returning home.

It was taking so long for the relief team to come and I felt so sorry for Chiyoko lying out in the heat that I decided to take her to the shelter built by our neighborhood association. It was very dark inside. The boxes of personal belongings that had been stored there had been broken by the blast, and the contents were scattered about the floor. Even if people had taken refuge here before the explosion, I doubt very much that they would have escaped injury. Tea chests were smashed and the zinc plates that had been inside them were twisted wildly out of shape.

I wanted to take Chiyoko to the relief camp, but there was nothing upon which to transport her, and it was too dangerous to try to carry her myself with the constant threat of enemy attacks. Anyway, she found it unbearably painful when I hoisted her onto my back. Around noon I decided to go alone and ask the relief team to come quickly. I made my way toward the camp but just before I reached it an enemy plane zoomed by and I dove for cover into a cave shelter in the hill. As I did, I ran into Mr. Miyahara. I remembered seeing him go by that morning carrying his wife on a stretcher, and I asked him how she was. He told me that she had died when they arrived at the camp and that he was going to cremate her body. Funeral pyres were already burning here and there among the ruins, and the sight was a dismal one indeed. Unidentified corpses were still scattered at the sides of the roads. Some of the corpses were bloated and partially decomposed, their features no longer human, and others were charred black. One person had died at the bottom of a well, presumably after being surrounded by the blaze and jumping in.

I brought two soldiers and a nurse back with me, and together we lifted Chiyoko out of the ditch and onto a tatami mat for treatment. The treatment consisted of simply spreading oil and talcum powder on the wounds and applying bandages. Her face was encrusted with what appeared to be black leaves, and the nurse spread the oil over these without attempting to remove them. I asked if she could receive treatment everyday. "It's difficult to say," the nurse replied. "We recommend that you carry her to the army hospital in Nagayo. If you take her as far as Ohashi you can catch one of the trains going out."

My mind became flooded with aching thoughts about what I should do: whether or not she could survive a trip to Nagayo, what kind of treatment she could receive there, and, especially, how I could possibly carry her to Ohashi.

I put Chiyoko back into the shelter and tried to feed her the rice porridge I had received from other survivors, but she wanted only water. She enjoyed drinking a hot cup of tea and then slipped into a deep sleep. I had to cremate the children's bodies before they began to decompose. I noticed that others were gathering lumber from demolished houses and using it to build funeral pyres. Just as I was thinking about this, Kinoshita, Mizogoshi and Moribayashi, my fellow workers at the Food Supply Headquarters, came to help me. I felt tremendously grateful to them.

We gathered scraps of lumber and made a neat pile. A lot of wood was necessary. We brought the children's bodies and placed them on the pile with Umito in the middle. I dressed Umito in a nightshirt of Michiko's I found in the ruins of our house and on top of that put his uniform trousers that had a tag saying, "Matsuo, 1-6" sewn on the lining. As a small consolation, I covered little Hiroto and Yukiko with blankets. We stacked another heap of wood over their bodies. I said a short prayer, lit the fire below their heads, and then passed the match to the four corners of the pile. There was a stiff wind blowing and so flames immediately began to lick up the sides of the pile.

> Under the scorching sun
> A fire rages,
> And in an instant
> Three cherished children
> Are lost in flames.

I sat down with a sigh of deep spiritual exhaustion and accepted a cigarette from one of my friends. Before long the three of them left me to myself.

The fire, lit around four o'clock, consumed the bodies by six o clock. But the embers were so hot that it was impossible to pick out the ashes of the children's bones. I was afraid that the fire might attract enemy airplanes and bring havoc to the other survivors, so I fetched some metal roof sheets that were lying about and covered the embers.

While waiting for the embers to cool, I went to the shelter

several times to check on Chiyoko. Her consciousness was clear, but she was very sick. She had no appetite and the diarrhea was as bad as ever. I decided to spend the night at her side. Thoughts of my three children and their ashes still lying out under the stars filled my mind.

12 August 1945

As soon as I woke up in the morning I went to collect the children's remains. I had placed a sheet of metal roofing at the bottom of the pyre, and now the ashes of the three skeletons were visible on it. The outline of Umito's body was in the middle and beside him the remains of his brother and sister. Of course there was no mortuary urn available, but I found an iron flower vase to use as a container for the ashes. Overwhelmed with emotion, I put all the ashes together and appeased my sadness in some small way by using a whole bolt of white cotton cloth to wrap the vase.

Chiyoko was still in a state of discomfort. The other survivors cooked porridge for her but she refused to eat it. These people from our neighborhood were very kind to us. I took a moment from my vigil over her to go back and look at the ruins of our house, a wooden bungalow built below the road. Debris from the houses to the front and sides were piled on top of the collapsed house; it was utterly unsalvageable. As I stood there, two officials from the office where I worked came to inquire about my family, and they urged me to bring Chiyoko into the city for treatment as soon as possible.

As night fell, Chiyoko seemed to have more pain and discomfort than ever, and she asked me repeatedly to take her to the hospital in Nagayo. I was torn between taking her to the Food Supply Headquarters, which had been converted into a relief station, and taking her to Nagayo outside the city.

13 August 1945

I decided to take Chiyoko to the Food Supply Headquarters for treatment, and then to her parent's home in Yanohira. I felt that going to Yanohira and letting her join her relatives was more in keeping with her real wishes than going all the way to Nagayo and risking her life. I thought that she would be particularly happy to be with her mother, who had always treated her with special affection. I borrowed a cart found earlier in the ruins by the neighborhood association and had Chiyoko lie on it with a quilt underneath and blanket on top. We departed early in the morning to avoid the chance of an air raid. Chiyoko was in good spirits.

From Shiroyama-machi to Komaba-machi everything was reduced to ashes. I noticed many unclaimed bodies, charred corpses of children frozen in a running posture, and blackened carcasses of horses and cows. The gutted ruins of Urakami Cathedral and Urakami Prison stood desolately in the wasteland. In Hamaguchi-machi I came upon the ruins of the steel works and arms factory. The bared metal frames of the buildings were twisted and crumpled; even the ferroconcrete chimney of the medical college was contorted. There was simply nothing left standing, not even a telephone pole, and not a scrap of wood had escaped the all-consuming conflagration. On the sites of private homes as well as factories, all that remained was dirt, stones and metal scraps. The amount of metal was particularly astonishing. At the Shinto shrine in Sakamoto-machi, one of the two stone entrance arches had toppled over and only one pillar of the other remained standing. The two huge camphor trees inside the grounds were reduced to obscure black stumps, and the main building and adjacent offices of the shrine had vanished. We proceeded through the wasteland, musing that the Funamoto family, our relatives in the area, had probably all been killed. On the way an air-raid alarm was sounded, but there was no place to take cover and we braced ourselves to die together. Chiyoko developed diarrhea again. The metal wheels of the cart made the ride extremely rough for her. She seemed to be feeling very ill. I pulled the cart gently, reducing the vibration as best I could.

Both Urakami Station and Nagasaki Station had been destroyed. After proceeding beyond the latter we finally entered areas that had escaped total destruction. But even there, the houses were only shadows of their former selves, their roofs, doors and windows broken by the explosion.

At last we arrived at the entrance to the air-raid shelter beside the Food Supply Headquarters. I had heard by this time that it was the air-raid shelter, not the office building, that had been converted into an army relief station. I brought Chiyoko into the shelter and she received treatment there, but the men in charge seemed reluctant to admit people not connected with the army, rather offering to carry Chiyoko by stretcher to the relief station to the north (Takaki Clinic in Kago-machi). In any case, they told us to wait until the air-raid alarm was lifted. We had arrived at the shelter around noon.

Chiyoko wanted tea, but fortunately she also sipped the porridge made by a helper in the shelter. She expressed gratitude politely to everyone who spoke to her, making a good impression even on me. She asked again and again if the air-raid alarm had been lifted. We felt very little fear because Nagasaki was already in a state of ruin, but the relentless wailing of the sirens was extremely annoying. We could do nothing but wait. Chiyoko's anxiety was understandable, but there was no other choice because people were forbidden to pass along the streets while the air-raid alarm was in effect. Time continued to pass, and while we waited Chiyoko suffered two or three attacks of diarrhea. At about four o'clock in the afternoon, Chiyoko's father suddenly appeared. It was completely unexpected. After taking care of Michiko in Yanohira, he had gone to Shiroyama-machi to look for us, but we had already departed. Unfortunately there was a power failure in the shelter when he came, and he had to take care of Chiyoko by candlelight. He had a backpack on over his shirt. He was a strong, reassuring figure.

The air-raid alarm was lifted at about five o'clock. I brought Chiyoko outside and put her back on the cart, and we set off toward Yanohira with a friend named Midori. We stopped at Takahashi Hospital on the way to obtain a cardiac drug, and then, moving along as carefully as possible, finally arrived in Yanohira at dusk. I asked Chiyoko if she was alright and she replied, "I'm fine," but she spoke in a strangely coquettish manner with her lip turned up and her teeth exposed.

She was overjoyed to see her mother again and to share her grief about the loss of the children. Michiko was sleeping in another room and apparently doing well. For the first time in what seemed like ages we were able to sleep on tatami mats in a house. During the night, however, Chiyoko began to talk deliriously. She spoke so clearly that at first I thought she was fully conscious. She sat up and tried to get out of the tent-like mosquito net. She seemed to be hallucinating because her utterances were mostly about the cart upon which she had been riding all day. "Just when I want to get some sleep," she said, "the neighbors come along and disturb me. They are sitting in the field now and calling to me to come over." Suddenly her tone changed and she spoke as though actually addressing our neighbors: "Hiroto is dead, Yukiko is dead, and Umito is dead too. Yes, yes. A stranger came and took the cart. He's an impostor so please go and get it back!"

14 August 1945

In the morning Chiyoko was normal again and she seemed in good spirits. She urged me to return the cart, so I left Yanohira and pulled it back to our neighborhood in Shiroyama-machi. When I arrived I found Kino, Urakawa and the others still living in the shelter. I tried to clean up the remains of our house a little but it was as good as impossible. I only managed to retrieve a few bed quilts and a box containing documents. It was terribly hot. I was exhausted by this time, and I decided to spend the night in Shiroyama-machi and to return to Yanohira at dawn.

In the early afternoon, Kazuo Nagao came to bid a final farewell to Umito. He had been Umito's closest mentor and friend, and very kind to both Umito and Hiroto. He had told his family before leaving that he was going to collect the ashes of "my younger brothers." This was how he felt about Umito and Hiroto.

Now that he was here and willing to help, I decided to dig out some of our belongings and to have him return with me to Yanohira. I had intended to stay in Shiroyama-machi overnight but thoughts about

Chiyoko were bothering me, and seeing Kazuo made me change my mind. This sudden burst of new energy was perhaps a premonition.

The most important thing I had to carry was the iron vase containing the children's ashes. On the way we were fortunate enough to meet two soldiers who were friends of Kazuo. They offered to carry our things as far as the Municipal Girls High School on the cart they were pulling, and so we arrived in Yamohira much more easily and quickly than I had expected. It was about 7:30 p.m.

As soon as I entered the gate my sister-in-law exclaimed: "Where have you been? Chiyoko is dying!" I ran into the house without even thanking Kazuo and rushed to Chiyoko's side. I was shocked to see how deranged she had become. It was dark, but the lights in the house could not be switched on because an air-raid alarm had been sounded. She was sitting up in the faint light and muttering as though explaining something, but I could not understand a word she said. As she spoke she reached out and tried to pull us towards her. When she pulled me close to her side I felt that she trying to embrace Hiroto or Yukiko. She was struggling with all her strength.

During the morning she had been in good spirits and was her usual self, but her condition had gradually deteriorated in the afternoon. She had asked for tomatoes, but they could only give her green tomatoes because there were no ripe ones on the vine. She took one of them and said, "This is for Hiroto," but when she put it down it rolled a few centimeters and she frantically grabbed it and hid it at her side. She also said quietly: "I am going to be another war death."

Later, Michiko came to the bedside and I said to Chiyoko, "Michiko is here now," but she did not seem to understand and continued to mutter to herself. She was probably suffering from brain fever; the pulling and tapping movements she made with her fingers were very similar to the ones Umito had made. She spoke with her lower jaw protruding and her lip rolled up, and we could not make out what she wanted to say. Since this deranged state did not subside we forced her to lie down, and the tranquilizer administered by her father seemed to take effect. Soon she was facing downwards, and I could hear the heavy breathing of sleep. Her legs were cold and so we placed several quilts over the lower part of her body. I remained at her side, watching. It was dark, all the lights being out because of the air-raid warning. She was so quiet that I lowered my ear time and time again to listen to her breathing. But soon I realized that her breathing had stopped. It was nine o'clock at night. Chiyoko and I had married when she was still only eighteen years old, and we had spent eighteen years at each other's side. Waves of emotion welled up inside me and tears spilled down my face. I slept at her side that night for the last time.

15 August 1945

My wife and three of my children were dead now, and today Chiyoko's body had to be cremated. I had not reported the deaths of the children to the police after cremating them in Shiroyama-machi, and I wondered what I should do now. Hearing that a makeshift city office had been set up near Nagasaki Hall, I decided to go there. A city official filled out a damage certificate for me, but at nine o'clock the police had still not arrived. When they finally came an air-raid alarm was sounded and we had to take cover. After an agonizing delay, I finally received the four death certificates and was instructed by the police to cremate Chiyoko's body in the playground at Irabayashi Elementary School. I returned to Yanohira and enlisted the help of Kazuo, Chiyoko's father and Chiyoko's sisters in carrying my wife's body to the school by stretcher. At the playground there was a hole where previous cremations had been carried out, the white ashes of human remains still in it. A large number of corpses had apparently been burned there together. We chose a site on the side of the playground near a sumo wrestling ring and potato patch. We used lumber that had been piled up after the demolition of buildings to make a firebreak, and built a stack for Chiyoko's cremation. It was a miserable irony that the knowledge I had gained from cremating my children's bodies a few days earlier came in handy now as I supervised the construction of the pile.

We could hear the sound of a radio in a nearby house. A broadcaster was telling everyone to gather because a very important announcement was about to be made. Since the explosion of the bomb I had neither listened to a radio nor looked at a newspaper. I had heard rumors about the Soviet Union's entry into the war and the escalating attacks on Japan, but it all seemed to be happening far away. I had had no time to reflect on the fragile state of the Japanese forces, and so now I imagined that this "important announcement" would be a declaration of war on the Soviet Union.

After erecting the initial stack of lumber, we lifted Chiyoko's body up onto it, piled up still more wood, and then set the stack on fire. Under the scorching sun, the blaze engulfed the wood and Chiyoko's body. Soon strains of *Kimigayo*, the Japanese national anthem, sounded from the radio, no doubt marking the beginning of the announcement. The announcement itself, however, was impaired by static and I could not understand what was being said. A little later some people came into the playground to cremate a body, and I asked them what the announcement had been. They told us that Japan had surrendered. I asked again in disbelief, but the answer was the same: "Japan has announced its surrender." I broke into tears. How can we surrender after all this!? What did my wife and children die for!? It was all for nothing! If we were going to surrender then why did we not do it sooner? It was just a matter of five or six days, and now nothing! Thoughts like these were rushing through my mind when another group of people arrived. They claimed that there had been too much static on the radio to understand the announcement fully, and that it was probably a declaration of war on the Soviet Union. This statement reassured me and helped me settle down somewhat.

It was unbearably hot. Kazuo drew some water and brought it to us. Chiyoko's body was gradually burning, but more firewood was needed. We carried lumber and added it to the blaze. Chiyoko had been a big woman and so it took a long time for her body to burn. We drank water and sprawled out on the weed-covered ground. The time came for Kazuo to leave for his regiment. As he went I could not find words enough to thank him. Midori came along and gave us pears to eat. At one point an enemy airplane flew overhead and we dove face down onto the ground. We continued our vigil until late afternoon when the fire finally reduced Chiyoko's body completely to ashes.

I found a clean flowerpot and used it as a container for the ashes, which Chiyoko's sisters helped me collect. The amount was equivalent to the ashes of the three children combined. We poured water over the ashes before trying to pick them up, but they were still extremely hot. By the time we finished, the sun was beginning to set. I held the flowerpot in my arms as we walked home. I could feel the heat penetrating my chest, and it made me nauseous. The grief I had been repressing so hard suddenly came to the surface, and I had to clench my teeth in order not to cry out hysterically. When we arrived home I wrapped the flowerpot in white cloth and placed it on the alcove in the main room beside the iron vase containing the children's ashes.

The statement about Japan's surrender had, in fact, been true.

22 September 1945

I am immersed in anguish from morning to night. If I could forget about everything it would be fine, but fretfulness, pessimism and disgust drive me into thoughts of death. Michiko's sluggish recovery irritates me and I think to myself that it would have been easier if she too had died. On the other hand, I think about how excruciating this must be for a child. What is she thinking as she lies awake staring upward with wide open eyes? There is unfathomable sorrow in those eyes. She lies in agony, with her mother, brothers, and sister dead, not knowing if or when her own injuries will ever heal.

(Postscript) My daughter's injuries refused to heal for many weeks thereafter, but at the end of November, when she was finally able to move to some extent, the two of us went to live in the mountain village of Sasa near Sasebo, Nagasaki Prefecture.

(Atsuyuki Matsuo is the author of the poetry collection *Gembaku Kushu*. Prior to his death in 1983, he lived in Hongochi-machi, Nagasaki.)

An Aspiration for Peace

Senji Yamaguchi

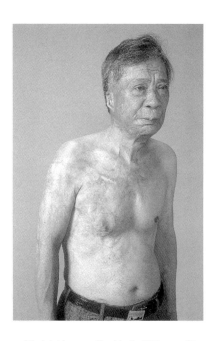

The keloid scars suffered by Senji Yamaguchi

Property of the Nagasaki Atomic Bomb Museum

August 9th, 1945. A thin layer of white cloud stretched across the summer sky, and a caressing breeze was blowing from no particular direction.

Mr. Yamashita, my team leader, ordered me to help dig air-raid shelters instead of my usual job of making gauges. Shelters were being dug throughout the city in a great hurry. At this rate, the whole field beside the factory in which we worked would soon be a maze of cave shelters. Most of us were working in the scorching heat with our shirts off. I was also covered in sweat and dirt. Four or five workers were allotted to each shelter, and several shelters of about four meters square in area and two meters deep were nearing completion.

"We'll finish it before lunch. There's only a little left to go," said one of my companions. We sang a song and heaved our shovels in time with the rhythm.

Suddenly, a bluish-white light flashed in my eyes.

I do not know how long I was unconscious, but when I came to my senses I was lying in the hole with the shovel still grasped in my hand. I stayed there in a daze for several minutes before I noticed something very strange. The companions with whom I had just been working were gone. I tossed away the shovel and stood up. The surroundings had completely changed. There were people scorched black and sprawled out on the ground glaring upward, and others face down on the ground as though sleeping. I glanced over at the factory and was shocked to see huge columns of fire shooting up from it. I climbed out of the hole, only to be astonished even more by what I saw. A kaleidoscopic vision of people running this way and that appeared before my eyes. There were people trudging down to the Urakami River and others running away with their clothes still smoldering.

Without thinking, I too began to run toward Urakami River, stepping over dozens of corpses as I went. I reached the river and jumped several meters from the embankment into the water, and then swam frantically. I do not know how I got to the other side or how I managed to climb the steep embankment. The village on the other side of the river was inhabited by a large number of Christians who made their living by farming. Their houses were shattered and blown to one side, and fire was already darting up from the debris. I was almost suffocated by the heat and smoke as I fled from the village, but I followed the other people running toward the hillside, dodging the flames that sometimes threatened to engulf me. I ran with all my might but still seemed to make very little progress because I stumbled again and again.

Passing a demolished house near the foot of the hill, I noticed a young woman trapped in the ruins and struggling desperately to free herself. She was flapping her arms and crying for help, and the fire that had broken out in the debris was on the verge of consuming her. None of the people running by, including myself, responded to her cries; fleeing from the conflagration was the only thought in our minds.

I arrived at the foot of the mountain and began to climb. There was no path and I had to cut my way through the bushes. As if to rub salt into a wound, plants slapped my face, wrapped themselves around my legs, and obstructed my progress. Nevertheless, I scaled hills and crossed valleys.

After two or three valleys I finally arrived in an area where no fires were burning. A group of people had gathered here: people sprawled on the ground with faces smeared in blood, people begging for water, and children crying hysterically. Utterly exhausted, I looked for a place to rest and sat down on the ground with my back to a big rock. I was barefoot and wearing only a pair of under shorts. The voices around me crying for water made me long for a drink too. Almost all the people had third-degree burns on their faces, arms and chests. Their faces were swollen up beyond recognition, and their slit-like eyes and white teeth protruded in stark contrast. It was impossible to distinguish men from women. After seeing these people I finally took notice of my own body. My hands, chest, and abdomen were scorched and swollen like the other people, but oddly enough it did not surprise me. Four or five blisters the size of candies had formed on the backs of both my hands.

(After that I was carried to the Naval Hospital in Omura for treatment.)

The sound of the car engine disappeared into the evening light.
Then morning came.   My father had already risen, and my
blankets and pillow had been straightened out.

"Drink up," he said as he pressed a medicine cup to my lips.   I
nodded and took two or three sips of something thick like porridge
from the cup.   My throat felt as though it had become narrower.

When I finished drinking, I heard the voice of an adult sobbing
in the bed beside mine.   When I moved a little in response, a stabbing
pain darted through the back of my head.

It was unbearable and I cried out.   My father leaned over me
and asked, "What's the matter?" several times in my ear.   I lifted my
bandaged arm slowly and tried to point to my head.   He seemed to
understand but caressed the bandages over my forehead.   His hand
felt as hard as rock.   I wanted to shout, "Not there!   It's the back of
my head!"   But I could only cry in vexation at being so bound and
fettered.

Suddenly, the clattering sound of the cart carrying medical
instruments echoed in the room.   This sound elicited a unanimous
groan of pain from the injured patients.

Soon the stench of rot and infection wafted on a warm breeze
and filled the room.

"It's over.   It's all over," said one of the nurses, trying to
reassure a patient.   The agonized groans of the injured mingled with
the metallic clatter of the medical instruments.

My turn for treatment arrived.   Three doctors and five or six
nurses peered at me, and my father stood back in silence.   "Kill me!
Please kill me!" I cried out instinctively as one of the nurses held up a
pair of tweezers to peel off the gauze patches.

The gauze was stained with pus that should have been absorbed
by the oilpaper and bandages.   Wielding the tweezers, the nurse lifted
the edge of the first patch and then ripped it off in one swift movement.
I gasped and a fierce pain wracked my body as though I had been cut
with a knife.   Two patches, three patches... I began to lose
consciousness and the sense of agony reached a plateau.   Now the

pain caused by the removal of a single patch was no longer perceptible. The patches were lodged deeply in the charred and swollen flesh right down to my eyelids, and the nurses tore them off one by one. Skinless pale-colored flesh was visible where the patches were removed, and bright red blood trickled from my face, chest, and abdomen onto the rubber sheet spread out below me.   By the time the patches on my back were being removed I had fallen into a state of stupefaction and my voice was gone.   The doctor wiped around the wounds carefully with alcohol, and then spread another disinfectant over the exposed areas themselves.

I sighed in relief when the treatment was finished, but noticed that my father was whispering something to the nurses.   One of the doctors overheard and came to look at the area of my body at which my father was pointing.   He cut something open with a pair of scissors, but it did not hurt very much.   Something cold was pressed into the skin on my head.

"It is best to keep the bandage in place," said the doctor.   "A bedsore formed there because he had a high fever for so long."

"Doctor," said one of the nurses as she wound a bandage around my arm, "this patient has developed blotches too."   Without understanding the significance of this, I looked at my arms and noticed I had several pea-sized purple spots on the unburned areas of both of them.   The doctor nodded and then turned away to continue his rounds, and I fell asleep soon afterwards.

On the evening of that day I began to feel sharp needle-like pains.   At first I thought they were due to the treatment I received that morning, but they became so intense that I complained to my father.   "I feel a prickling pain all over my body," I said.   He ran his hand over the bandages on my back asking, "Here?   Here?" at different places.   The frustration of not being able to explain made me want to strike him with my bandaged arm.   I burst into tears instead and he stood over me helplessly for a while before dashing off to the nurses' station for help.   He reappeared with a nurse at his side.

"What are the tears all about?" the nurse inquired with a smile. Her smiling face enraged me and made me cry even harder.   "My whole body is prickling with pain!" I blurted, still in tears.

"All right, we'll get rid of the pain for you," she said as she left my bedside and headed toward the nurses' station. She returned with another nurse carrying a large metal tray and a rubber sheet. Convinced that she was aware of the cause of the problem, I gazed at the equipment out of the corner of my eye.

The nurses unwrapped my bandages and exposed the oilpaper below them when suddenly scores of plump white maggots fell out onto the rubber sheet. I started in surprise and my tears let up instantly. The nurses also jumped back in shock, and my father was stunned. Hundreds of the maggots were squirming and crawling on the rubber sheet. The nurses poured creosol over my wounds and washed off the remaining maggots. My back was infested too, and I could feel them moving about on my buttocks.

"Bastards!" I muttered to myself.

"It won't hurt anymore," said the nurse as she rewound my bandages. I laid back feeling relieved but it wasn't for long. "They're still some left," I said to my father, but he rejected my complaints, saying that it was probably the places where I had been bitten before the treatment. I insisted, though, and finally he rose from his chair and went to call the nurses again.

"You're pretty spoiled, aren't you?" said the nurse, arriving at my bedside before my father did. She held my hand and smiled.

"Seriously, it still hurts," I said.

"Does it hurt that much?" she retorted, looking at me with a disdainful expression on her face. "The pain you had before is not going to go away that easily."

"O.K., forget it," I blurted out in anger, unable to keep the tears from welling up.

Without saying anything, the nurse began to unravel the clean bandages that she had applied only minutes before. She obviously thought that what she was doing was a waste of time. She lifted up the oilpaper but no maggots fell out.

"There are none left," she said in a tone of voice that showed she had no intention to look under the gauze patches.

"There are still maggots in the wounds!" I cried out desperately.

"Mr. Yamaguchi," she said to my father as she turned to leave the room, "please keep him just as he is for a moment." She returned with a tray containing tweezers and other instruments, and proceeded to remove the gauze patches from my abdomen and back. However, there were no maggots to be found and I felt very embarrassed. She stood looking over me, her warm breath brushing against my wounds.

Just when I shouted, "ouch," she thrust the tip of the tweezers in front of my eyes and showed me a tiny maggot before I could scream words of abuse.

"There are a few small ones like this hiding in the flesh," she said. My anger shifted quickly to the maggots.

She picked out five or six of the insects and the tweezers took fragments of flesh with them, but I endured the pain in silence.

When she finished I said, "thank you" in a low voice.

"You'll be fine now," replied the nurse, glancing at my father as she rewound the bandages.

By the next day, about 34 maggots of various sizes had infested the burned skin around my right ear.

Maggots caused great suffering for all the injured patients.

(While experiencing a variety of physical and mental suffering after that, I graduated from the Nagasaki Industrial School and later joined the movement to ban atomic and hydrogen bombs.)

From around October that year, we began to hear frequent reports about deaths due to atomic bomb disease. These reports left an indelible impression on the hearts of all the atomic bomb survivors, particularly those still hospitalized, who were overcome with the desolate feeling that their turn was next. And sure enough, atomic bomb disease took one life after another in Nagasaki hospitals.

Twelve of the people who had been hospitalized with me died one after another during the period from July to December 1956, and by the beginning of 1958 there were only four of us left. All of the people who died – the young woman who had been looking forward to marriage, the student who was soon to graduate, Mr. Kaneko who worried about the fate of his children and cried out their names to the very end – had each had a glimmer of hope for the future.

Mr. Shirai, who was in a terminal condition, wrote a letter to his wife of eight months from his hospital bed. The tears that welled up from the depths of his being stained the pages:

"Dearest Masumi,

It is out of love that I write to you now. Please forgive me for concealing the fact that I am an atomic bomb survivor. The effects of acute leukemia have damaged all my internal organs. My abdomen is swollen like a frog's belly, making it difficult even to breathe. I have no appetite. In fact I haven't eaten anything in five days. I don't know how many days more I can continue to live. The doctors only shake their heads in silence. I pray quietly for your future. Please marry someone who has not been exposed to the atomic bombing, and please win back the happiness that I took from you. That you will find happiness as soon as possible is my one, all-consuming wish. I can no longer find the strength to write.

Jun'ichi Shirai, Room No.3"

While Mr. Shirai languished in the hospital, Masumi was working as a live-in maid at an inn in Nagasaki. She looked forward to her weekly visit to her husband's bedside and probably never expected to receive such a letter. Mr. Shirai died the evening after he entrusted delivery of the letter to a nurse. Masumi rushed to the hospital after hearing that her husband was in critical condition, but she did not make it to his bedside in time.

He had lost his parents and both his brothers in a flashing instant on August 9, 1945. Now, with a white cloth over his face and his young wife weeping by his side, he added another name to the Shirai family death list.

One evening a week later, I visited his grave to pray.

Excerpt from the memoir *Heiwa wo Negau* ("An Aspiration for Peace")